Helping Kids
Find a Place in
God's Story

dwelling

FAITH ALIVE®
Christian Resources

Grand Rapids, Michigan

Printed in the United States of America.

We welcome your comments. Call us at 1-800-333-8300 or email us at editors @ faithaliveresources. org.

ISBN 978-1-59255-682-3

10 9 8 7 6 5 4 3 2 1

Contents

1 Welcome to the Real World

When Dorothy arrives in the Land of Oz, she looks around at the new world she's entered and tells her dog, "Toto, I've a feeling we're not in Kansas any more." You may feel a bit like Dorothy as you realize that the children you're teaching are growing up in a different world than you did!

If we lived in a vacuum-packed, hermetically sealed world where biblical values are taken seriously, teaching church school might be easy. But we don't. Incoming messages delivered to impressionable kids today come through television, movies, electronic games, music, print, the Internet, and other cultural realities that do not reflect our faith.

Just what are those messages? Old certainties are fading. Reason can't be trusted. It's important to challenge and question common perceptions. There is no absolute truth—reality and truth grow out of your own perceptions and experiences. This worldview—called "postmodernism"—describes the predominant attitudes and values of the world our kids live in. They know no other world.

If we did still live in a Bible-centered world, perhaps people of all ages would not be pigeon-holed and labeled by the era of their birth. But that's not reality either. "Boomers," "busters," and "Gen Xers" are labels for people born during certain periods in recent history. Because of the experiences they've been through, each generation looks at life in different way than previous or succeeding generations. Life is messy that way!

The children in our church programs have labels too: they're known as Generation Y (aka Millennials), children born between 1982 and 2001. Their younger brothers and sisters, Generation Z or the Net Generation, were born after the catastrophic events of 9/11.

So who are these kids you'll be teaching—and what are they like?

- For the most part, these children are are cherished. With readily available birth control measures, parents can choose whether and when to have children. And when they do, their kids are generally protected and fussed over!

- Today's kids are knowledgeable and comfortable with technology, at ease in cyberspace. They live in a global village, communicating easily online with children around the world.
- They are used to multitasking as they move between screens on their computer while listening to their iPods and texting their friends on cell phones. For these kids, thinking has become a nonlinear activity—they feel very comfortable with random bits of information.
- Children today are extremely tolerant of a variety of opinions, cultures, and lifestyles; personal freedom to choose is a value they hold passionately.
- They want to *experience* things before they learn about them (in religious terms, this means that they come to your class in search of a "God experience"—not just a series of stories, facts, and concepts).
- Kids' "fake" detectors are very sensitive! You'll need to earn their respect—it's not automatic. Morality tales that feature "goody-goody" characters are out—*real* is in.
- Today's children and young people can be wonderfully idealistic and unselfish if presented with the right challenges.
- Kids and teens have a pick-and-mix approach to spiritual beliefs. They're looking for a spirituality that reflects their own experiences.

Generation Z is growing up in the shadow of Generation Y. Anything that can be said about Generation Y also applies to this younger generation, only more so! These kids have never known a world without computers, without "war on terrorism," without DNA evidence and maps of the human genome, without discussion of gay rights. Reality and fiction are blurred as special effects in entertainment become ever more sophisticated. Their world bears little resemblance to the world we grew up in.

Of course, behind each of the labels we've talked about is a child uniquely created and loved by our great God. Some children conform to the tidy labels and descriptions we give them as though they were poster children for their generation. Others are totally unlike their labels, marching to their own drummers. Most fall somewhere in between.

These are the children who'll come to your classroom each week. We're committed to helping kids in this complex culture and global world find their place in God's family, dwell in God's love and grace, and grow in their faith. Our task is a challenging one. Thank God—the loving, creative, very real God of *all* generations—for knowing and loving the children in your group before they took their first breath. In a changing world, that's a message that will never change. It's our hope for generations to come.

2

Real Kids, Real Families

It all starts with family. Family is everything to a child: it's a place to belong, to be loved and cared for, to learn and grow.

Family is where a child first forms relationships and figures out whether people are to be trusted. It's where a little one learns to talk and walk. Within families, children learn social rules, obedience, and negotiating with others. It can also be where children first experience violence, neglect, and rejection. What they've learned will travel with them as they walk through the door into your classroom.

Since family is so important to a child's faith development, we should be aware of what's happening in the family these days. Some of the statistics do not paint a very pretty picture. Here are some trends in families you should know about:

- One out of every six households in North America moves each year, often away from the support of extended family.
- Two out of three preschoolers live in homes where the TV is usually left on at least half the time, even if no one is watching.
- Computers, the Internet, chat rooms, email, Instant Messaging, cell phones and text messaging are used heavily in most households, diverting time from family activities.
- According to the Urban Institute, children make up approximately 39 percent of the homeless population (2000). In 2004, 19 percent of all children lived in "food insecure" households. Children make up nearly 40 percent of all emergency food clients.
- Thirty-three percent of children born today are born to unwed mothers; single-parent families are statistically the poorest families in society.
- Half of all children [in the United States] will witness the breakup of their parents' marriage. Of these, close to half will also see the breakup of a parent's second marriage. Forty percent of children growing up in America today are raised without their fathers—statistics that are similar for Christian and non-Christian families (www.nappaland.org).

You can find many more troubling statistics online—statistics that detail declining educational standards, increased violence within families, financial and job-related stresses that impact children, and time crunches that squeeze families almost beyond their endurance.

Other family factors, while not necessarily negative, also impact your classroom. Immigration is increasing the number of children for whom English is a second language and families in which parents are struggling to establish themselves in a foreign culture. Increasing urbanization means that kids may not be as connected to God's creation as they have been in previous generations. More children have both parents in the workforce, which means that more children spend time with caregivers other than their parents.

Get in touch with the family situations of the children you teach. You cannot assume that the kids in your classroom will have had a good breakfast before coming to church or that their parents will take the time to reinforce a session truth by doing a project at home. Some children in your class may have parents who share custody, making it hard for the children to attend church and Sunday school regularly. These are realities in your children's ministry programs.

On the other hand, it's also important not to lose sight of the positives in today's family. A recent survey published by sociologists at the University of Maryland indicates that parents, both mothers and fathers, are spending more time with their children than they did forty years ago. Parents today are also more aware of their children's needs—and they're responding accordingly, even if it means that other parts of their lives such as leisure activities, civic responsibilities, and friendships with other adults get short-changed.

In an encouraging survey done by the Australian Childhood Foundation, four out of five parents reported that maintaining a positive relationship with their children was a high priority, and the parents who responded were looking for information on strengthening these relationships. Most parents want to do the right thing.

It's not easy to be a parent in a world that isn't family-friendly. Behind every child who comes to your church school program are parents who recognize the importance of their child's spiritual nurture and faith formation—and they are looking to you for help. What a privilege to partner with families in these changing times! With the power of the Holy Spirit, you'll have the joy of helping children dwell in God's love and take the next steps in their faith journey.

3 Ages and Stages

Five-year-old Sarah loves to sing "Jesus Loves Me" at the top of her lungs. Eleven-year-old Joe is much too cool to do the same, but he willingly accepts and acts out a role during the "Living into the Story" step each week. Eight-year-old Cedar, new to church, asks what the words *Holy Spirit* mean; Amanda, a first grader, thinks it means that Jesus is a beautiful dove flying over the church. Sachi, a sixth grader, does a great job of explaining the Trinity using the example of three states of water.

Each of these kids is exhibiting characteristics of his or her age and developmental level. It's so important for teachers to understand that children develop in an orderly and predictable progression—the stages they go through have been studied and documented by experts in child development for years. We're all familiar with this example of a developmental pattern: a baby generally rolls over before she begins to creep, creeps before she crawls, and crawls before she walks.

While physical growth and development usually peak when a person is in his twenties or thirties, some other ways of growing continue well beyond that point. Psychologist Jean Piaget was a pioneer in studying child growth patterns in *mental* (or cognitive) development. Another psychologist, Erik Erikson, described *emotional* development as a series of challenges human beings must master from infancy through late adulthood. Lawrence Kohlberg studied *moral* development: how people change over time in the way they make moral choices. And James Fowler, who studied *religious* development, used the groundwork of Piaget, Erikson, and Kohlberg to show how people, beginning as very young children, grow in faith.

The chart on page 10 illustrates the theories of Piaget, Erikson, and Kohlberg in a very simplified way as it applies to the children using the *Dwell* curriculum in your church school program. (We'll take a more detailed look at faith development in the next chapter.)

	Piaget: Stages of Cognitive Development	Erickson: Stages Emotional Development	Kohlberg: Stages of Moral Development
Infancy-2 years	The very young child learns and grows through using the senses—hearing, seeing, touching, tasting.	*Trust vs. mistrust.* A child asks (and finds out): "Is this world a good place for me?"	
Ages 2-6 years	The child learns and grows by developing language skills and using lots of imagination. She still thinks concretely, with no ability to think logically or abstractly. Everything is black and white—no grey!	*Autonomy vs. Shame:* "I do it myself" is the child's motto, but he feels a sense of shame if he fails. *Initiative vs. Guilt:* "I want to try that" says the child, wanting to imitate adults. Again, she'll feel guilty if she can't measure up	What's right in a child's eyes is what authority figures say is right. ("I will obey because I don't want to be punished.")
Ages 6-11 years	The child gradually acquires an ability to use logic in situations that are real and observable, but this logic does not yet apply to abstract concepts. (Children in this stage enjoy learning facts, are very literal in their interpretations, and see issues in terms of right and wrong.)	*Mastery vs. Inferiority:* "Can I do what's expected of me?" "How do I compare to others?" are questions kids in this stage are seeking to answer.	There is more than one way to view right and wrong. ("I will obey because it will help me get on in this world.")
Adolescence	Young people are now able to think in abstractions and use logic to solve problems. Teens are beginning to develop their own framework for viewing life.	*Identity vs. Role Confusion:* "Who am I? I feel very self-conscious."	A growing understanding that moral choices can be judged by intentions behind the choice, not just on a black-and-white definition of right and wrong. ("I will do the right thing because I want to be thought of as a good person.")

By studying the work of theorists like Piaget and Erikson and others—and putting the pieces together—we begin to catch glimpses of how children learn and respond at various stages in their growth. Jesus said, "Let the little children come to me and *do not hinder them*" (Matthew 19:14). Understanding the particular ages and stages of the kids we teach will help us to encourage and challenge children in their growth and avoid unknowingly putting stumbling blocks in the way of children's emerging and deepening faith.

Check out www.dwellcurriculum.org to find out more about kids in the age group you're teaching.

4
Stages of Faith

Parents and grandparents watch in wonder as the newest family member takes her first steps, prattles her first word, grows a mouthful of teeth, lets go of a sibling's hand and scampers off to preschool or kindergarten on her own. Wonderful milestones on the journey to adulthood!

With praise to God for the Spirit's work in us, it's the same way with faith development! Children are born as spiritual beings. They grow in faith from the time they're tiny—and their faith matures and deepens into adulthood and old age.

How do the seeds of faith first get planted in children's hearts, and how does their faith grow? What is the nature of children's faith when they walk into our classrooms? Are there common characteristics that we can identify and understand?

Yes, says James Fowler, theologian and author of *Stages of Faith* (Harper and Row, 1981). Fowler's work is considered foundational in the area of faith development. He describes the following stages that define the path of faith growth:

Stage 1: Primal or Undifferentiated Faith (birth-2 years)

Infants are totally dependent on their caregivers to give them a sense of the world: Is it a safe place? Can people be trusted? Who am I? Am I worthwhile, cherished, and loved, or am I bothersome and a burden? For young children, these are very fundamental understandings of the world and the people in it. They are essential ingredients for developing a connection to God—and the beginnings of faith formation. The kids in your classes have just passed through this first stage, and their approach to faith has been shaped during this critical period.

Stage 2: Intuitive Projective Faith (2-6 years)

Children in this stage are beginning to express themselves independently. They're acquiring many new language, motor, and social skills, often through imitation. Too young to think logically or abstractly, these kids use imagination to interpret their world. Their faith is based squarely on the messages and attitudes they're exposed to in their families.

Since kids at this stage will believe almost anything adults tell them, and since it takes little to stimulate their imaginations, teachers have an awesome responsibility to introduce them to a loving, caring God. Firm and loving boundaries help a child feel secure. Symbols, rituals, and stories appeal to children's imagination and play a huge role in their faith development.

It's important to realize that children at this age do not understand abstract concepts that are presented as mere words and ideas. For instance, the phrase *love each other* means little to a child unless it's associated with concrete actions such as making a get-well card for a senior. Nor do object lessons—analogies based on abstract comparisons—work very well. Stories well told, followed by wondering questions (check out chapters 14 and 24) are much better avenues for stimulating the imagination and inviting young children into the mysteries of our faith.

Stage 3: Mythic Literal Faith (ages 6-12 years)

As their world expands, kids in this stage are increasingly influenced by many adults other than parents. These children use logic to process multiple viewpoints; they're eager to ask questions and make sense of the world they're experiencing. They're also beginning to understand the concept of time, and their motor and social skills are becoming more fine-tuned as well.

Kids this age are beginning to understand the difference between imagination and reality, which has implications for their faith development. They're seeking to create a world of beliefs they can be sure of—for the most part a black-and-white world with few greys. But because they are beginning to be able to take another person's perspective, they're starting to see the world as God may see it. Although they can't yet understand how their own experiences, wishes, and needs influence their view of the world, they do begin to see that stories from the Bible have something to say to their own lives—"Jonah got a second chance; maybe God will give me second chances too."

Regardless of the ages and stages of the children in your group, one thing is sure—God's story, told with all of the awe and excitement you can muster, will speak loudly to their growing faith. So will God's message of love and compassion, which you model to them as you extend Jesus' unconditional acceptance: "Let the children come . . . and do not hinder them, for of such is the kingdom of God."

5
Families First

Where are the seeds of faith first planted by the Holy Spirit? Within the family! Children first learn what it means to be a child of God by being part of a faith-filled family. That's according to God's plan—just read God's instruction to the Israelites in Deuteronomy 6:6-7: "These commandments that I give you today are to be on your hearts. Impress them on your children. Talk about them when you sit at home and when you walk along the road, when you lie down and when you get up."

Admittedly the family God was talking about in this passage was much different than today's family. The children of Israel thought of family in layers. First was one big family, all the descendants of Abraham. Families also belonged to a tribe, and within each tribe were clans—today we call this "extended family." Finally there was the family itself—grandparents, parents, children—living together in the family compound. All parts of this layered Israelite community shared responsibility for raising the children, imparting values, and passing on the faith.

Today's nuclear family, though, is still entrusted with passing on the faith. The church partners with the family in this process—in some ways taking on the role of the large extended family of biblical times.

Here are some ways for you, a teacher or leader in children's ministry at your church, to help parents nurture the seeds of faith:

- *Communicate with the parents of the children you teach.* The more contact there is—by phone, letter, email, notes, personal visits, or informal chats at church—the more parents will consider you their partner in faith nurture. What a gift you are giving that family!

  Children's take-homes in *Dwell*—Show and Share papers, Storymarks, or magazines—are another tool you can use to communicate. They're great ways to encourage parents and pass along to them ideas for nurturing their children's faith. Each unit of *Dwell* includes a letter in hard copy or an email version to send families as you begin a new unit. Consider sending it in the mail with a personal note, or clipping to it a card with your contact information as you send it home with the children. In addition, there's a set of God's Big Story cards with suggestions for activities families can do to bring home the truth of each session. For more on these resources, check out www.dwellcurriculum.org.

Look for other creative ways to communicate with families. One teacher called each parent at the beginning of the semester to introduce herself and share her hopes and dreams for the group. This initial family contact also gave her opportunities to find out more about her children's fears and anxieties as well as their gifts and strengths. You could also set up an email list and send occasional updates on what's happening in your group. Let parents know you'll be praying for their children, and encourage them to contact you with questions or problems.

- *Make it a priority to create a safe community in your classroom.* Faith grows best when it is planted in good growing conditions. In the best families, children are accepted without reservation and treasured just as God cherishes them. Their unique abilities are affirmed; they are gently guided in behavioral expectations and offered forgiveness when they fail. Your classroom cannot replace a family's total love and acceptance, but it can be a safe and sheltering place where each child dwells in God's love and where the family's love and teaching are reinforced.
- *Tell your story.* When families tell stories about things that are a part of their identity, children get a sense of family history and family values. Our hope is that children will want to be part of God's big story, so sharing stories of your own faith walk—its joys and struggles, its hopes and, yes, its failures—communicates to children that they are part of a larger family, a community that shares its story too (see also "Sharing Your Story," chapter 35).
- *Extend an invitation to visit your classroom.* Aubrey Schneider, children's director at Celebrate Community Church in Knoxville, Iowa, writes, "We held our first Family Festival in March where all of the kids' families were invited to attend Kidzone on a Sunday morning. We had a skit, sang songs, had activities and contests . . . the families loved it. We had treats, balloons . . . very festive." Aubrey figures she'll do this twice a year as a treat for everyone. What an encouragement for parents to know that others are sharing in the care and the nurture of their children's faith!

6 Community Matters

Do you think of yourself as "just" a staff person or volunteer in children's ministry? Think again. A recent study by the Commission on Children at Risk says you are a hero! You're a hero because you are meeting a child's inborn need to have quality relationships with key adults who model and pass along spiritual values.

This commission involved thirty-three respected authorities on children's health and welfare who studied statistics and reports and conducted their own research into the rising rates of mental illness, behavioral problems, and emotional difficulties in the lives of children.

Their 2003 report, *Hardwired to Connect: the New Scientific Case for Authoritative Communities*, suggests that such deep-seated problems arise because children lack connections to people and to moral and spiritual teachings. Scientific evidence exists, they say, to prove that children are "hardwired" for close attachments with other people, starting with their parents and extended family, and moving beyond family to the broader community.

Children who experience strong relationships both within their families and in the larger community will be healthier emotionally and physically. They will be less predisposed to antisocial behavior and will grow up to be better parents and members of society.

This secular commission also strongly believes that we as human beings are created to seek a connection with the transcendent. In other words, we need God! This is no surprise to those of us who love and serve our great God. As Augustine said so many years ago, "Our hearts are restless until we find our rest in you."

As we've seen, today's culture puts a lot of pressure on families. A 2003 survey done by the Barna Research Group found that 85 percent of parents of children under age thirteen believe they have the primary responsibility for teaching their children about religious beliefs and spiritual matters, and 96 percent believe it's their job to teach their children values. Here's the kicker, though. "Related research revealed that a majority of parents do not spend *any* time during a typical week discussing religious matters or studying religious material with their children" (Barna Research online).

Add to that sobering statistic the fact that extended families are no longer a reality in many children's lives. And that other institutions in the broader community that used to have a lot of influence are also under a great deal of stress. The good news is that the church and its ministries are hugely important to children. We are part of a larger community that can help children connect with others and connect with God.

In your work with children, you are meeting a deep need as part of what the Commission on Children at Risk calls an "authoritative community" with enormous benefits for children. Here are the characteristics of an "authoritative community" applied to a church community:

- You are part of an institution (the church) that deliberately includes children and youth. There are not very many other institutions like it left in today's society.
- You value children. Like Jesus, you value children enough to spend time with them.
- You nurture children, establishing clear rules for their security while building caring relationships with them.
- You represent a different generation, one from whom children can learn.
- You may be a volunteer, not a professional teacher—you are giving of yourself.
- Your work has a long-term focus, your teaching has eternal consequences.
- You're sharing with children what it means to be a "good person" (in Christian terms, a Christ-follower)—someone who spends his or her life for the benefit of others.
- You are encouraging children to develop spiritually and morally.
- You respect people of all kinds and affirm their dignity; you are teaching children what it means to obey Jesus' words to love God first and your neighbor as yourself.

(*Note:* Read more about this commission by doing an online search using the words "Commission on Children at Risk" or "Hardwired to Connect.")

When children are baptized, the congregation challenges the faith community to become part of their "authoritative community." Thank you for accepting that responsibility!

7

Dear Teacher. . .

Dear Teacher,

My mom tells me I'm going to Sunday school again this year. That's cool. Here's what I hope will happen:

- I hope you'll love me like nobody's business. You don't have to be the greatest singer or storyteller or craft expert ever, but you do have to love me lots. I hear that's what Jesus did, even when his disciples disappointed him.
- I hope you show me that Jesus is living in your heart and that he's changed your life—and I hope you want to tell me about it. If it's real for you, I'm going to want to try it too.
- I hope you know how to joke around a little. My mom says that laughter is the shortest distance between two people. What are you going to do if the bottle of glue tips over in your purse or the craft doesn't turn out the way it's supposed to? When we laugh together I feel good—and I feel good about being in Sunday school.
- I hope you can go with the flow. Once my friend came to Sunday school so sad because his grandma had just died. That day we just talked about heaven and made paper flowers to put on her grave. We all felt better afterward.
- I hope you don't think my faith is not as good as your faith. I know I've got lots to learn because I'm just starting out on this faith journey thing. But Jesus said grown-ups should have faith like a kid's, and that must mean something. Can you show me that there's a kid inside of you?
- I hope you'll expect the best from me. Even if I sometimes complain and whine, I'll be pleased that you think I can grow to be the best I can possibly be.
- I hope you'll understand where I'm coming from—please try to look at the world from a kid's point of view. And remember, I don't have all the thinking and physical skills grown-ups have.

- I hope we get to move around and do cool things, instead of always sitting and listening. Moving, talking, looking, drawing—that's what helps me learn!

There's more, but I'll bet you get the idea. Deep down, I'm really glad you want to help me learn more about God and more about me. Thanks for being here . . . hope you learn something too!

Love,

Your "kid" for the year!

8

What Does It Take?

So . . . you're warming to the challenge. Great! But you still have a few questions about what this commitment takes. Quick now! Think of a memorable teacher you've had, someone who impacted your life positively. Why is this teacher one you'll never forget? Write down three of his or her most memorable characteristics:

1. ______________________________

2. ______________________________

3. ______________________________

If you're like most people, you'll write down things like:

- She really cared about me!
- He had a great sense of humor.
- He had a passion for the Bible—he really made it come alive.
- She challenged me to become a better person.

What's not on your list? If you're like others, it's probably things like:

- He could recite Psalm 119 from beginning to end.
- She kept great attendance records.
- Her classroom was always neat and tidy—everything had its place!

It's usually the *character* or personal qualities of a memorable teacher we recall, not his or her specific skills—or even the academic content that person taught. And that's the way it should be, for character begins in the heart and spirit of lives transformed by God's grace. And that's exactly what your teaching is all about.

A wise person once said you only need three loves and two skills to be a good teacher.

1. Love God.
2. Love the ones you teach.
3. Love what you teach: God's Word.

1. The ability to communicate effectively.
2. The ability to create a community in your classroom.

Notice that both the "loves" and the "skills" relate to connections. If you're connected to God in your personal life and if you earnestly desire to connect with the children entrusted to you, you *do* have what it takes!

Nobody can teach you the three loves—they're gifts of grace from God, gifts that will keep growing in you, thanks to the work of the Holy Spirit. (Check out chapters 32-34 for ideas on nurturing your own spiritual growth.)

Effective communication and community building skills are things you can learn, however. (Check out coming chapters for more about discipline, questioning, storytelling, understanding the theory of multiple intelligences—as well as suggestions for building community, affirming diversity, and staying in touch with families.)

We hope you're not thinking, "Yikes! I can't do that." Remember Paul's advice to Timothy, a young and inexperienced teacher: "And the special gift of ministry you received . . . keep that ablaze! God doesn't want us to be shy with his gifts, but bold and loving and sensible" (2 Timothy 1:6, *The Message*).

If you believe that God is asking you to teach children, then you do have what it takes. God delights in watching us grow and learn and pass on the good news to others! And when you respond to that call, someday, somewhere, some grown-up children of God will remember and tell others about a memorable teacher they once had—you!

9

Diversity, the New Reality

There you are, your group gathered round as you conclude the story of Noah and the ark. Cedar, an earnest eight-year-old, responds with this question: "Why would the Great Spirit want to destroy Mother Earth?"

Obviously Cedar has grown up listening to different stories than you are telling. And Cedar is not the only child in your class with different ideas, especially if you are using the curriculum in an outreach context. You may be working with kids who don't even have a concept of God, or whose family faith practices directly contradict the Christian message.

Before we consider how to answer Cedar's question, we need to honor two principles in this context:

- First, God has given *parents* the task of teaching their children spiritual truths, whether they recognize this or not. If we honor this principle, we must show respect for children's beliefs (even if we personally consider them strange). To undermine parental teachings by pointing out how wrong they are—or how they contradict God's Word—is to dishonor the trust parents have placed in us to nurture their children on their spiritual journeys.
- Second, God loves every child and calls each one into a life-giving and loving relationship. God's desire is that all children will come to know Jesus as Lord and Savior. Our role as leaders is not to convince children of the truth—that's the job of the Holy Spirit. We don't need to be God's sales force! The church's role is to proclaim the good news in such a way that children gladly hear it and receive it. God will take care of the rest. (For further help with leading children to Jesus, see chapters 38 and 39.)

Even if all your children come from a church background, you will find wide variations in their knowledge and beliefs. In our postmodern world there's increasing divergence in basic Christian beliefs. In a sense, your job has become like that of a missionary, even if you are working right here in North America. Here are some ideas for teaching God's word in a multifaith and multicultural context:

- *Focus on what you have in common*, not on the differences your children bring to the group. We may find Cedar's language strange, but he is asking about God and God's creation. You might want to answer Cedar's question by saying, "The way we tell the story here at our church is that God . . ." and proceed to share each story of faith using the religious language of our tradition. This allows kids to see that their story is reflected in the one true story of the whole world, namely the gospel.
- *Learn more about the children you teach*, and, especially about the beliefs and faith practices of their families. The more you know about them, the better your relationship with them will be. As well, remember that children are very adept at reading body language. If they ask a question, and your body suggests surprise, shock, or anxiety—even if your words say otherwise—they will be less likely to listen to your answers. Knowing more about other cultures and faiths makes us less likely to be taken by surprise—and we'll be better equipped to find commonalities and answer children's questions more intelligently.
- *Connect with families*. You are a faith-nurturing partner with the families of the children you teach. If you build relationships with them, they are more likely to trust you and listen to you. If some parents don't attend church, a simple phone call can open the door to better communication.
- *Use lots of wondering questions* (see chapter 14). Wondering questions rely less on information that a child already knows and more on a child's thoughts and feelings. Questions that ask kids to wonder provide a level playing field for children who don't know as much about the Bible—and you'll learn much from their answers! (Check out chapter 13 for questioning techniques that encourage children to think about their answers.)
- "The truth is out there—somewhere" has become a guiding principle for people who are seeking spiritual certainty. But *you know and have experienced God's truth. So share it!* Be confident but humble—after all, faith is a gift of grace, and our message should come from grateful, not arrogant, hearts. (Check out chapter 35 for ways to share your own faith story.)
- *Pray!* Pray as you prepare your session; pray for each of the children in your group; pray as you open your mouth to teach; pray when you are not so sure about how to handle a sensitive situation. Pray at all times and in all places, and the God of wisdom will keep your heart and your mind in Christ Jesus.

10

The Immigrant Experience

God must love immigrants—the Bible is so full of them! Abraham was an immigrant. So was Joseph. Ditto for the people of Israel, who emigrated from Canaan to Egypt to Canaan to Babylon and back to Canaan.

"Treat the foreigner the same as a native. Love him like one of your own," God commands the Israelites (Leviticus 19:34, *The Message*). The writer of Hebrews urges, "Do not forget to entertain strangers, for by so doing, some people have entertained angels without knowing it" (13:2).

Hundreds of thousands of people with hope in their hearts for a better life immigrate every year, often with only rudimentary English skills. Children of such immigrants may become part of your group. How will you welcome them?

The following will never completely prepare or train you for this experience, but here are some insights that may help.

Immigrant children have more to sort out than language issues. For example, statistics say that more than 40 percent of Canadian immigrant children live in poverty. Cultural differences make a difference too: some cultures train children to be quiet and listen, so that children may not feel comfortable participating in discussions and debates, or working in groups. These kids may be perceived as "different" by the other children, and thus may feel lonely or excluded. If they have come from a war-torn country, they could be suffering from post-traumatic stress. Differences in customs of food, dress, greeting, traditions, and norms all add to the difficulty an immigrant child faces in making herself at home in your classroom as an eager, active participant.

We have much to learn about ministry with immigrant children. Perhaps we cling to a few stereotypes: "Asian children love math" or "Hispanic children are good at soccer." Perhaps, deep down, we believe that North American culture is superior to other cultures—and inadvertently demonstrate this belief with our body language. We might even catch ourselves giving privileges to children from the dominant culture because they act as though they are entitled. Perhaps our rudimentary knowledge of what life is like in other countries leads us to say or do things, without knowing, that offends these children. All of these cross-cultural misunderstandings stand in the way of welcoming and "treating the foreigner the same as the native."

Here are some building blocks that will help you welcome children from immigrant families (and perhaps, in so doing, entertain angels unawares).

- *Examine your attitude.* Children from immigrant families may add to your teaching load, but they are also God's gifts to you and the other children. Through them, God is giving you an opportunity to learn, grow, and practice spiritual gifts, and to receive the gifts they bring.
- *Become a model of welcoming behavior.* Practice hospitality and encourage everyone in your group to do so too. This is a wonderful opportunity to emphasize Jesus' great command to love our neighbors as ourselves. The result? A greater sense of community.
- *Find out all you can about your students*—the circumstances of their immigration, their family structure, where the child attends school, whether he's happy to be here. Such knowledge will help you meet that child's needs more readily.
- *Don't assume anything.* A child with Latino features may trace his roots for several generations in your country—he's more North American than Latino. The child who can't say "I need to use the bathroom" in English may someday be a Nobel scientist. The quiet, compliant child may be harboring distressing and violent thoughts. The child who challenges you may be expressing himself in a way that's normative for his culture.
- *Learn at least a few phrases in the child's language*, and teach them to the children in your group. Doing so indicates your desire to establish a relationship. (Don't overuse them, however . . . the child may feel patronized or embarrassed if you do.)
- *Use alternate ways of communicating.* While words are important, studies show that our bodies communicate more than our speech. Posture, facial expressions, simple sign language, and expressive gestures are all effective ways to communicate.
- *Use activities that incorporate a number of different intelligences.* (See chapter 15 for more information on Multiple Intelligences.) When children use pictures, movement, and music to respond to a story or to express themselves, language becomes a smaller issue.

- *Pair the child with another child* in your group who has a gift for hospitality. He or she can mentor the newcomer, learning much in the process.
- Using old Sunday school resources, *create a word book or flash cards*. Cut out pictures of Bible stories and characters and glue them into the book or onto the cards, with words printed underneath. In the same way, you could create a "survival" manual of the church building and property, pairing photos of important features (bathroom, drinking fountain, fellowship hall) with matching words to help children become more comfortable at church.
- It is not your responsibility to analyze or treat depressed or disturbed children. However, if you are aware of a need, *consult with church staff* or an education committee member, asking them to step in if appropriate. Church members may also be good resources for helping you understand how best to teach and reach kids from immigrant families. (If you have an ESL specialist in your midst, be sure to tap that person's knowledge and sensitivity too.)
- *Invite involvement from the children's families*; they may be willing to share food, pictures, and stories with your group. Again, be careful about singling out just one child for this attention. Consider projects that involve other families as well—sharing family backgrounds and traditions across cultures.
- *Focus on what you have in common* and build on that. All children have the same needs—to be loved, to learn, to feel appreciated and needed, to experience God's grace and forgiveness. Build on that!

God blesses us when we extend ourselves for the good of others. That's what love—and teaching children—is all about.

11

Building Community

Wouldn't you know it! The week you make twenty-five popsicles as a treat for your kids (more than enough!), twenty-six children show up. The next week, just to be sure, you make thirty Rice Krispy bars and eight children get to share them. The kids are happy, but you are left scratching your head.

One of the facts of life, hard to accept but true nonetheless, is that coming to your group is optional for many children. Families these days are stressed and busy; parents don't always understand the vital importance of their kids' spiritual nurture; single parents may be sharing custody of their children. Sunday school is not the only game in town—sports events, birthday parties, and community celebrations are often scheduled for Sunday mornings too.

We may not like how this plays out, but deal with it we must. How do you cheerfully handle the unpredictable size of the group from week to week? How can you encourage children who come consistently to welcome those who come only occasionally? How can you stay in touch with kids whose attendance is sporadic?

A good place to begin is by recognizing and accepting reality. In an ideal world, children would wake up their parents on Sunday morning and clamour to be taken to Sunday school. Face it, that doesn't happen! But whoever does show up deserves to hear God's message presented in the best way you know how. Remember that Jesus promised "Where two or three come together in my name, there am I with them" (Matthew 18:20). Two people—that's you and just one child. Isn't it wonderful to feel sure that the Maker of the universe will show up for a meeting with just you two!

Nevertheless, you'll still want to put lots of energy into encouraging everyone to come *every* time. Here are some suggestions from seasoned teachers:

- *Prepare welcome bags* for each first-time visitor to take home. Fill the bags with some or all of the following: a welcome letter; information about the program; a brochure or card with contact information (names and phone numbers of teachers and leaders, name and address of the church, website address, and anything else that will be helpful to parents—even a photo of yourself); a fridge magnet with a blessing or poem; a simple gift such as pencil and pad, coloring book, or Bible story book. (Stamp your gifts with the church name and information.)

- *Be warm and welcoming.* In a culture that presents children with options, they'll choose to come to a place where they're recognized and appreciated. Help them feel included within the first few minutes of arriving. Welcoming kids by giving them nametags is helpful too. Ask kids to put on their tags as soon as they arrive to help you call everyone (especially the sporadic members of your group) by name. Consider appointing a greeter (perhaps another child) whose job it is to give visitors and newcomers such basic information as where the restrooms and drinking fountains are and to introduce them to other children.
- *Arrive early.* Newcomers are often early birds because they want to scope things out before making a commitment to stay. If you're waiting for them with a warm smile and cheerful words, you'll make a great first impression. Leaders are also role models, so monitor your words and attitudes: no "insider" jokes that might exclude some children; no "teacher's pets." Explain routines that may be new or unfamiliar to some children, and keep language simple. Watch for signs of confusion that call for clarification.
- If you have a core group of older kids who come each week, consider starting a "Kid2Kid" partnership program. *Pair a regular attender with a child who's new* or who comes only occasionally, and encourage that child to be responsible for welcoming his partner, phoning him if he misses a session and looking out for him.
- Whenever you divide kids into small groups, *be sure a newcomer is paired with an outgoing, friendly child.*
- Many churches ask leaders to *make home visits* part of their Sunday school programs. A home visit is usually quite informal, something as simple as a short introduction on the doorstep, delivery of a welcome bag, and encouragement to parents to contact you with questions. There are so many benefits to these short, friendly visits—you'll get a more intimate perspective on each child's home life; you're giving parents the gift of knowing someone else cares about their child; and children will feel good knowing that they are special enough to deserve a visit from you!

- *Communicate regularly.* Communication specialists suggest that people need to hear a message many times in order to really remember it. There are many different ways of communicating beyond the standard note sent home with the child. Consider the following ideas: once each quarter, send a postcard in the mail; add a Sunday school blog link to your church website, and have leaders post what's been happening in their classes; mail or hand deliver the children's take-home paper to families, adding a personal note; email families with occasional updates on what's happening; email children with an occasional "Hi, how's it going?" message, reminding them of something that is coming up; take photos and create a class poster to hang in the fellowship room; call parents on the phone just to touch base.
- *Set up special events*—Bible Character Sunday (kids dress up as their favorite Bible characters); Sundae Sunday; Bring a friend Sunday. Passing on information about these special events gives you an extra reason to communicate with sporadic attenders.

When you are intentional about building community, God is pleased. Do your best and ask God do the rest.

12

Step by Step—Session Prep

Now you're a leader—kids will be coming through your door looking for inspiration, affirmation, knowledge. That's a tall order. Maybe you've never taught Sunday school before—you've probably never taken a short course in education theory either. And maybe you don't know the first thing about lesson plans. Your heart is in the right place, but you feel woefully inadequate. Where do you start?

On the other hand, perhaps you have done lots of teaching, but you're new to *Dwell*. How do you use your past experience to inform this new personal challenge? Maybe the image of a juggler will help. . . .

Amazingly, the balls, the flaming torches, or the rings a juggler flings always seem to land in his hands. It looks like magic—but it's not! After hours of preparation and practice, the juggler acquires an uncanny knowledge of where all the airborne pieces are. His hands are in the right place at the right time to catch each one. He'd be making a giant fool of himself if he just flung the rings into the air, hoping they'd land back in his hands. In fact, he wouldn't be a juggler at all—he'd be a clown.

While leaders do bring fun into the classroom, they're not clowns. Their fun has a serious purpose, and it's carefully planned to land in square in the hearts of children. It's no accident—and it's not magic either. Purposeful teaching comes from thinking through a session step by step and carefully planning for a successful presentation to achieve specific goals.

As you put your session together, step by step, consider these important details. It can become as easy as 1-2-3:

1. Start at the Beginning

Do you begin your lesson prep by checking out step 1, asking yourself, "What do I need to do first?" If so, you've missed a crucial detail or two. Check out the stuff at the top of the page, right under the session title—the Scripture passage, focus, and faith nurture goals.

Immerse yourself in the Scripture passage, using the "Getting into the Story" reflection as an opportunity to nurture your own faith as you explore the Scripture that's the vital nine-tenths of the iceberg below the surface of your teaching. Read the verses, and then read them again slowly. What surprises you? What do you notice that you never noticed before about the passage? Is God telling you anything personally? We teach out of the fullness of our hearts—what's in *your* heart as you read this story? Grab a cup of coffee, a pen, and notebook, and prepare to spend some time with God. (And don't forget to check out the teaching ideas that will help you invite your kids to dwell in God's Story too.)

Check out the focus statement too . . . maybe even memorize it. It summarizes the important truth you pray the children will take with them from your teaching. Also spend some time with the faith nurture goals listed there—they're intended to guide your teaching, keeping it focused! These goals reflect things you'll want your group to experience, discover, and do as you seek to nurture their faith in a way that responds to the nudge of the Holy Spirit.

2. Get Ready to Share God's Story

Now you're ready for Step 1, "Gathering for God's Story," which involves coming together to greet one another and greet God in worship. It often begins with an opening question or activity that helps prepare kids for hearing God's story. It usually includes praise, prayer, and an occasional activity. Start by listening to the songs on the *DwellSongs* CD and learning them well. Karen DeBoer, curriculum writer and editor says, "The best way you can teach a song is by being prepared. Learn by listening. That means playing the songs you'll be leading over and over again during the week—on your computer, in the car, on your iPod or CD player. Then teach the kids the same way—by playing the song, listening to it together, then singing along."

If your leader's guide suggests an activity, make sure you have the materials and instructions for the kids ready before they arrive.

Step 2, "Entering the Story," is designed to help you present the Bible story to your kids—it's the heart of the session! God is inviting the children into the story through your presentation. You'll want to have all the people and props prepared and ready to go. (If the story presentation is a drama, be sure to get the script to your presenters earlier in the week so they have time to prepare.) For more on storytelling check out chapters 24 and 25.

3. Get Ready to Live into (and out of) the Story

For the last two steps of each session, your role will be that of nurturer and facilitator rather than storyteller or presenter. But that takes planning too. In Step 3, "Living into the Story," kids revisit the story you presented in Step 2, retelling it in a creative way of their own, wondering about it, and allowing it to sink into their memories and hearts. Spend some time ahead of each session thinking about how you can best lead this process, inviting the kids to imagine themselves into the stories to discover God's ways and God's love.

Step 4, "Living Out of the Story," will help you plan ways to bring the story back to the children's own lives, putting them in touch with familiar situations in which God is speaking to them as God spoke to the biblical characters in the Scripture story. You will get to know your students well, which puts you in a great position from week to week to plan for meaningful ways to live out of God's story together.

As you prepare to teach a session, you may realize that you have better ideas for presenting the story and nurturing your kids' faith than the session plan provides. Follow your heart and trust your instincts! For example, you may be presenting the story of Jesus healing Jairus's daughter to children who've lost a friend or classmate to death. If so, they'll undoubtedly have needs and questions that won't be covered in your leader guide. Depart from the plan, pray with them, and address their questions of the moment—you know and love the kids in your group more than any curriculum writer ever can.

The last word on "prep" comes from the apostle Paul. Listen to his words to Timothy: "Stay right there on top of things so that the teaching stays on track . . . the whole point of what we're urging is simply love . . . " (1 Timothy 1:3a, 5a, *The Message*).

13 Questions about Questions

What are the best kinds of questions to stimulate kids' imaginations and nurture their faith?

The answer comes in the form of other questions—answer the following as fast as you can:

1. What is your name, and how old are you?
2. How long have you been teaching children at church?
3. What do you like about teaching children?
4. What challenges you most about teaching children?
5. How has working with children impacted your spiritual life?
6. If you could make sure kids take away one message from Sunday school for the rest of their lives, what would it be?

Did you find that it was easy to answer the first two questions, but that you needed progressively more time to answer the rest? That's the way it should be! So you don't want to ask children factual questions exclusively (like the first two above) for which they'll come to think the answer should always be *Jesus* or *God*.

The questions you just answered demonstrate three kinds of questions you should always try to use during the course of your session:

- *Questions for information* (1, 2): These explore the content of the story and are generally factual questions, such as Who healed the blind man? How many people did Jesus feed? Name three of Jesus' disciples.
- *Questions for explanation* (3, 4): These dig deeper into the content, inviting children to draw inferences and process ideas. What was unusual about Abraham's journey? How did Peter's life change after he became Jesus' follower?
- *Questions for application* (5, 6): These invite kids to ponder the importance of a story or session focus in their own lives. If you were in the boat with Jesus and the fishermen, would you have been frightened by the storm? What kinds of situations are frightening to you right

now? Can you trust Jesus to care for you when you're frightened by things around you?

If you plan your questions before each session, you can make sure to address each of the different levels of your children's understanding.

How can I encourage children to take the time to think about answers?

Your body language can encourage children to think more deeply. As you ask a question, keep your eyes moving around the room. (If you focus just on one person, the rest of the children will often tune out.) After asking a question, lower your eyes to the floor or table for at least fifteen seconds and remain silent. By not making eye contact, you are giving thoughtful children the opportunity to think through the answer, as well as giving the "Jesus is the answer" kids time to reconsider or think more deeply.

What do I do when kids offer an answer that is totally out to lunch?

Accept each answer as though it were a gift. When children answer questions, they make themselves vulnerable to teasing or laughing if the answer is wrong. So even if the answer is way off base, affirm the child's courage. An appropriate affirmation might be, "Good try" or "Thanks for thinking about that." Or you might deflect the spotlight to yourself by saying, "Maybe my question was hard to understand. Let me try that again."

Are there some questions I should never ask?

Never ask a question you would not be willing to answer yourself. You're a fellow traveler, not an inquisitor. And be careful about asking questions that pressure children to reveal more than they feel comfortable doing. When you want children to think about personal issues, respect their privacy by inviting them to answer the question in a journal. (Tell kids you will only read these if invited to do so.) Or suggest that they spend time thinking about their answers silently.

What if I don't know the answer to a question they ask me?

Say, "Good question! I don't know the answer, but I'm going to try and find out." By doing so, you're modeling the concept that the Christian journey is one of constant learning and growing—not one of knowing all the answers!

Now, here's one last set of questions for you: Who loves teachers and kids very much? Who is pleased to see God's kids struggling together to ask big questions? Who said, "Ask and it will be given to you; seek, and you will find; knock and the door will be opened to you"?

You know the answer to that one—it's *Jesus*, of course!

14 Wondering about Wondering

When is a question not a question?

When it's a wondering question.

But what's a "wondering question"? you're probably wondering. It's not so much a question as it is an invitation to ponder and reflect on a situation, a feeling, or an issue. Wondering questions give kids opportunities to express themselves without worrying about whether their answer is right or wrong. It's a marvelous, open-ended connection, linking the imagination to the spirit.

You'll find lots of wondering questions in *Dwell*, questions tailor-made to help your kids enter into the story, to imagine themselves in it, and to figure out what the story means to them.

Why place such a high value on stimulating kids' imaginations through wondering questions? Developmental psychologists have determined that imagination plays a central role in young children's growth and development. By using their imaginations, children formulate ideas about God, about adult roles, about how the world works. "The magnificent and untainted imagination of young children draws them toward the stories of the Bible," writes Ivy Beckwith in *Postmodern Children's Ministry* (p. 50). "They are easily persuaded to wonder about the power, love and mysteries of God." Thus much of a child's early spiritual life is rooted in the imagination.

But wondering questions aren't just for little ones. Older children and adults too grow through imagining. "Exercising our imagination in Bible study can make the characters of the story come alive for us, and may even help us sense the reality of God's love and grace in new ways," says Catherine Stonehouse in *Joining Children on the Spiritual Journey* (p. 212). She suggests that leaders dust off their imaginations as they prepare to tell God's story. "When we have been there in our imagination, the story becomes real to us and comes alive for the children as we tell it." So as you prepare to teach, wonder how you would have felt if you were there when this story happened. Wonder what you would have heard, smelled, seen. . . .

Wondering questions remind leaders and kids alike that we do not and cannot know everything. Faith is a mystery, and some questions can't be answered. "If I introduce children to a God who is so small I can explain everything about him, I am shortchanging the children," writes Bob Keeley in *Helping our Children Grow in Faith* (p. 50). "Part of the wonder of God is that we will never fully understand him." Wondering questions help us become comfortable with this reality ourselves, as well as teach children this important truth about life and faith. If kids know it's okay to ask hard questions, they'll be more comfortable exploring the boundaries of their faith later in their development as they begin to make their parents' and their church's faith truly their own.

Another value of wondering questions is the opportunity to delve beyond the world of right and wrong answers. If you only ask kids questions that have right answers, they'll tend to think only on a factual level. When we ask questions that require more thought, children become more creative and think more deeply about God's story.

Wondering questions promote dialogue because they level the playing field between adults and children. Statistics show that teachers in a school classroom may ask up to *four hundred* questions a day. How much time does that leave for children's questions? When we ask wondering questions, we encourage everyone to share their ideas, creating a richer community. Children's responses to these questions will give you insights into their personalities and their thinking. The ideas that emerge from their young minds and hearts may surprise you. We all learn and grow through pondering the meaning of Scripture passages, and wondering questions are ideal vehicles to ensure that this happens in your classroom.

Asking wondering questions may require some practice, and encouraging good responses may require some patience. Here are some helpful tips:

- Ask wondering questions in addition to the other three types of questions we discussed in the previous chapter.
- Note that answers to information and explanation questions in particular will help you ascertain that the children have really heard the story, ensuring that your wondering questions are based on information kids have internalized.
- Wondering questions invite children to take time to imagine and reflect. You will need to allow for periods of reflective silence, a significant goal of *Dwell*. If taking time for quiet reflection and

thoughtfulness is unfamiliar to the children, explain the wondering question/answer process well, emphasizing that there are no right or wrong answers, and that sometimes nobody will answer the question because they are thinking and responding to it in their minds. Emphasize that it's okay to be quiet for a while and respect everyone's need for time to think.

- Use body language that encourages reflection by looking down as you ask the question and waiting to make eye contact with the children for about ten seconds.
- Invite children to ask their own wondering questions too. Explain that one question may start them thinking about other questions, and that they are welcome to ask their own wondering questions.
- Be aware that wondering questions may send your carefully planned session into new directions—and time frames. That's okay! By asking wondering questions you are giving the Holy Spirit time and room to work. And following the Spirit's lead is sure to make for something good!

15

He's Smart, She's Smart

Sandy fidgets during story-telling time but loves to take center stage in a drama. Jeannie, on the other hand, listens with rapt attention to your story but shrinks if she's asked to perform. Jason really enjoys puzzles in the take-home paper but tunes out when your group sings. Su-Lin loves to draw and paint but often becomes disruptive during a reflective activity. What's that all about?

Well, it's all about multiple intelligences. Not only do children (and adults) have different personalities, they also have different ways (called "intelligences") they prefer to use to learn and solve problems. Multiple Intelligence (MI) theory suggests that there are many ways to be intelligent or "smart." A star hockey player may not be verbally gifted, but he's always in the right place to grab the puck and put it in the net. You might call him *body smart*. A budding artist may have real difficulty figuring out math problems, but her antismoking poster wins a national award. She's *picture smart*.

Here's a list of the eight intelligences (*Dwell* calls them "smarts") observed by researchers; see if you can associate each one with a child or children in your group:

- **Word Smart** (aka Linguistic Intelligence): sensitive to the sounds, meaning, and functions of words and language. Word smart kids learn through storytelling, writing, reading, chanting, and poetry.
- **Number Smart** (aka Logical-Mathematical Intelligence): able to discern logical or numerical patterns and reason through puzzles and problems. Number smart kids learn through counting, classifying, and puzzle-solving.
- **Picture Smart** (aka Spatial Intelligence): able to use visual impressions in creative ways, perceive and learn best through pictures and symbols. Picture smart kids learn through artwork, design, inventing, and creating symbols.
- **Body Smart** (aka Bodily-Kinesthetic Intelligence): good at controlling body movements and handling objects skillfully. Body smart

kids learn through movement, athletics, drama, and other physical activity.

- **Music Smart** (aka Musical Intelligence): able to produce and appreciate rhythm and pitch, appreciate the forms of musical expression. Music smart kids enjoy and learn through singing, playing instruments, rhythmic activities, and listening to music.
- **People Smart** (aka Interpersonal Intelligence): able to feel and respond to moods and motivations of others, sensitive to others' feelings. People smart kids like to lead, help, create community, and work in groups.
- **Self Smart** (aka Intrapersonal Intelligence): sensitive to one's own feelings and emotions, aware of one's own strengths and weaknesses. Self smart kids often prefer to learn independently, write in a journal, read, and reflect.
- **Earth Smart** (aka Naturalist Intelligence): sensitive to creation and what it teaches, aware of the interrelatedness of life, observant of natural rhythms. Earth smart kids learn by examining nature, being outdoors, observing growth and change, and linking natural phenomenon.

Although people (including you) generally have one or two leading intelligences (the way they learn best), each child in your group possesses all eight intelligences to one degree or another. So there's no need to create eight different lesson plans to reach everyone in your group!

However, if our Creator made us with such a variety of learning capacities, doesn't it make sense to encourage children to grow in faith through a variety of learning experiences and activities, thus honoring the image of God that's inherent in each of us?

Reaching each child you teach is a worthy goal and—good news!—it's attainable too. With some adapting by you, *Dwell* will help you plan and adjust your teaching strategies and activities in ways that are varied enough to reach the different intelligences represented by your kids. (You'll note that each activity in your leader's guide is labeled to show which intelligence(s) are primary for that step.)

Often the biggest obstacle to using this approach is the leader! Research shows that in a traditional classroom, teachers talk their way through 70 percent of classroom time. Obviously, that kind of teaching appeals most to word smart kids—and even then, they're not getting a lot of opportunities to use words themselves. Meanwhile, teachers are not reaching those who learn best through other kinds of smarts.

So don't ditch those fun activities and ideas just because you think you're not really "teaching." Check out the box below for examples of ways to *really* teach—and *really* learn! (Note that many of the activities appeal to several "smarts" at the same time.)

Aa

Word Smart: brainstorming, choral reading, word games, storytelling, journaling, making recordings of children's contributions, publishing a newspaper. For example, children might record their prayers for a sick member of the congregation and send it to her with cards of encouragement. Other "smarts" tapped in this activity:

Number Smart: classifying, sorting into lists, graphing, counting, creating and using codes, logic puzzles and games, arranging facts in sequence. For example, children might poll each other to discover who is their favorite Bible hero. Other "smarts" tapped in this activity:

Picture Smart: photography, creating models and dioramas, working with play dough and other art materials, using symbols, finding patterns, visualization exercises. For example, children might build the walls of Jericho with shoeboxes. Other "smarts" tapped in this activity:

Body Smart: creative movement, dramatization, pantomime, active games, crafts, cooking, using sign language, hands-on activities, stretching and relaxing. For example, children might go on a trust walk with a partner while blindfolded. Other "smarts" tapped in this activity:

Music Smart: singing, humming, whistling, listening to music, rhythm instruments, chanting and rapping, learning memory work in song. For example, children might clap a rhythm while learning a memory verse. Other "smarts" tapped in this activity: Aa

People Smart: cooperative group activities, peer teaching, board games, clubs, parties and celebrations, acting out roles, people sculpting. For example, children might work in small groups to develop a list of five questions for reviewing the story. Other "smarts" tapped in this activity: Aa

Self Smart: independent study, one-minute reflection periods, contemplative prayer, choice in activities, interest centers, journaling, private spaces. For example, children might be given a choice of writing in their journals or creating a piece of art as a response to the storytelling. Other "smarts" tapped in this activity: Aa

Earth Smart: nature walks, plants and pets in the classroom, discovery tables, experiments, nature posters for decor, recording observations from classroom windows, weather watch. For example, children might check out whether objects will sink or float in a tub of water before listening to the story of Peter's attempt to walk on water. Other "smarts" tapped in this activity:

16 Shortcut Smart

Multiple intelligence theory is great stuff. But maybe you're thinking, *Since I only have these kids for a short time each week, it might take me half a year to notice how they learn best.* Is there a shortcut? Yes! There are a few ways to help you determine children's preferences.

Dwell offers a questionnaire you can give kids at the beginning of the year to help you pinpoint their preferences. While this is a very simple and by no means definitive test (and it works better with kids who are able to read and write), it will begin to give you insights into how your children learn best.

Keep in mind that by administering this written quiz, you are using a word and number smart activity, which in itself is limiting. You could easily adapt the way you present this quiz to appeal to more than these two intelligences; for instance, you could orally list several activities as found in the quiz, then ask children to draw themselves doing their favorite activity (picture smart). Follow that by asking the children to act out their least favorite activity (body smart).

While you're at it, you should take the teacher's version of the quiz yourself as well. You'll find both versions at dwellcurriculum.org. Knowing yourself is a good foundation for teaching others.

For the first session or two, consider offering activity alternatives that kids can choose between (rather than having everyone do the activity suggested in the guide). Tailor your choices to a variety of intelligences, not just the primary one used in the suggested activity. For example, the first session of Marvel, unit 1, presents Jesus' parable of the Lost Sheep. Kids respond to the story by drawing a graphic novel/comic strip (picture smart kids will love this!). Alternatives you might offer kids would be:

- Getting together with a classmate to talk about the questions listed in the "Living into the Story" step (people smart).
- Journaling a response to one of the questions (self smart).

- Finding a song that fits with the theme of Jesus as our Shepherd (music smart) and creating motions for the song (body smart) to teach the class.

  Note the activity choices your children make and record them, adding this new information to what you learned about them from the multiple intelligences quiz.

As you assess your students, keep these points in mind:

- While most kids generally have one or two *leading intelligences* (the way they learn best), each child in your group possesses some degree of all eight intelligences. That's reassuring! No matter what you do, something will get through—the Holy Spirit will make sure of that.
- If you find that your group leans toward one or two intelligences, take advantage of their natural preference by choosing those activities deliberately when you find them in the session plan. Feel free to adapt your session plan, however, if a suggested activity is not likely to work for your group.
- If your group is all over the map, use this tip, passed on by a teacher with many years of experience. "You may not reach each child each week," she said. "But you can be sure to reach at least one child each week." To do this, gear your lesson plan each week to one particular child in your group. Step into that child's shoes and look at your session from his or her point of view, and choose an activity with him or her in mind. (There's another advantage to planning this way: the child on your mind will also take a place in your heart! You'll begin to pray for her, thinking of specific needs as you ask the Holy Spirit to watch over her and prepare her heart. What a gift this child receives!)

  By planning for a different child each week, you will plan and implement great sessions that will reach *all* of the kids entrusted to your care and nurture!

17 The Rest of the Story . . .

You've done your session prep, collected materials, and prayed for God's presence—and you're sure kids will love this session. If only that were the whole story! That's usually when Jake struts in and your confidence sinks into your boots.

Jake's in fine form today. Within a few minutes, your group is in turmoil. Much as you love him, Jake seems to bring disruption and confusion with him into your room. When you shut the door an hour later, you wonder how things could have gone so wrong. Is it your fault? Is there some technique you haven't learned that might have helped you maintain better control? Maybe you're even doubting yourself, wondering if you should be a teacher—maybe this isn't my gift after all!

It can be very discouraging, says Aubrey Schneider, children's ministry director at Celebrate Community Church in Knoxville, Iowa. "[Teachers] give of their time and energy to help teach our youngest members about Christ. They have one of the most important and unrecognized roles in the church. They aren't in it for the recognition. They love being around and teaching God's children, and to me, that is inspiring. But sometimes disruptive kids can be our biggest frustration on a Sunday morning."

What can you do to bring an impossible situation back into line? And how do you deal with children who have behavior disorders? We'll suggest a few tips and techniques, but before you delve into the how-to's of discipline, let's define what it is and why it's so important.

According to the dictionary, *discipline* is 1. A system of rules used to maintain control over people 2. Punishment; reprimand. If that's your idea of discipline, think again. In the dictionary (as well as in a Sunday school classroom), the word *disciple* comes before *discipline*. The root word for both is the Latin word *discere*, meaning *to learn*.

Learning, not punishment, is what discipline is all about. It's helpful to remember that the ultimate purpose of discipline is training and teaching, not justice or revenge. Your teaching focus is on the future, teaching alternative behavior—not the past, punishing poor behavior. Thus your attitude toward behavior that begs for discipline becomes one of disappointment and love, rather than anger and frustration.

Differentiating between *discipline* and *control* is also helpful for teachers. Classroom discipline is important not merely to maintain control and orderliness during a teaching session, but also to help children grow more Christ-like in their thoughts, words, and actions.

So perhaps a better definition of discipline, especially in your Sunday school room is this: *training children's hearts and minds to grow in a way that reflects God's image in them.*

Discipline is not an option. By recognizing its importance, you demonstrate that you love these kids enough to care about their future. God does that with us too: guiding and correcting us, watching over us as we learn and make mistakes with the gracious intent of conforming us to his image.

Here are two keys to effective classroom discipline:

1. Good classroom discipline comes from the heart—your heart.

   You may have heard that teachers need to carry a big stick (figuratively, of course). But that's not nearly as effective as possessing a big heart. Do you like kids? Do you respect their strengths and try to build them up where they are weak? Do you pray that the kids in your group will become all that God created them to be? Do you want to show them Jesus' love? Do you model spiritual habits you hope they will learn? Then you have the foundation for good classroom discipline, for creating an environment where children can learn.

2. Good classroom management is built on preparation.

   How about making your motto "prepare and prevent"—not "repair and repent"!"

   - Prepared teachers feel more comfortable and confident in their role. They're able to give the children more attention because they aren't spending precious minutes putting last-minute details together.
   - Prepared teachers know what they want to accomplish; their goals provide direction and momentum in the classroom.
   - Prepared teachers think about their kids as they plan the sessions, anticipating possible problems and making contingency plans.
   - Prepared teachers think about each child's needs and shape the session to meet these needs.

In other words, to be an effective disciplinarian, you need to discipline yourself too! To grow as Christ's disciple, you need to be ever learning and changing. Your goal for yourself and the children you teach is to share in Christ's holiness. And that's a whole lot better than carrying a big stick!

Check out chapter 29 for further help in pinpointing your areas of strength and weakness—and keep reading for more practical tips and suggestions.

18

Discipline—WWJD?

Your heart is in the right place and you've prepared carefully. So everything is certain to go smoothly, right? Not necessarily. As one experienced teacher put it, creating a disciplined environment to ensure optimal learning requires equal parts of technique *and* personality.

What about that personality thing? Teachers come in all varieties. Some are warm and nurturing, others are charismatic and energetic. Some are good storytellers but don't like singing; some love doing arts and crafts but feel less confident leading games and group activities. In the same way, some are naturals at creating a disciplined learning environment while others have to work at it. If you're in the latter group, don't lose heart. It doesn't mean that you shouldn't be teaching—you can be sure that God will use you.

One older teacher, reflecting on a Sunday school class he taught in his younger years, remembers it as a disaster. The kids seemed to run all over him, his plans ran amok, and chaos was the norm. So he was surprised when, meeting a former student from that class years later, the young man said, "I remember you! You were such a cool teacher. I loved going to Sunday school. And you really showed me Jesus' Spirit—you were so patient with us."

God works in mysterious ways! You may worry that the seeds you've planted will be choked out, but God, as always, is in control. When teaching feels more like hanging on for dear life than sailing on a lovely lagoon, these tried and true techniques shared by experienced teachers might help you restore quiet waters to your room:

- *Gear your teaching to children's attentions spans*, allowing about one minute per year of age for each activity. (Expecting a five-year old to listen to a ten-minute story without involving him in movement or response as part of the story time could be an invitation to trouble.)
- *Match your teaching to kids' interest level.* Bored or frustrated children inevitably look for something else to do, and usually that's not a good thing! Know the characteristics of your age group, and make sure your activities are varied and your vocabulary and expectations appropriate.

- *Clearly communicate a few basic expectations* to the kids—and then be consistent in enforcing them. You cannot assume children know what you expect, so state the things that are important to you at the outset. (Keep your list of rules short or you'll be spending all your time being a traffic cop instead of a teacher.)
- *Involve the group* by communicating "big picture" expectations and goals; then invite their cooperation in creating and observing rules. (For example, you might agree on a secret code that only you and the children know about—like "XYB" (examine your behavior)—that cues kids to check their behavior.)
- *Strike a balance between routine and variety.* Routines kids can count on, such as opening rituals, theme songs, and prayer times, give everyone a sense of security and add stability to the program. Variety in activities keeps everyone involved and interested. (So for example, vary the way you do your routine prayer time. Invite different children to lead the opening prayer—or supply motions to it. (Your *Dwell* session plans suggest a variety of activities, while always following the same step-by-step format that helps kids know what's coming.)
- *Respect children's individuality* and preserve their dignity. Shouting, physical restraint, and singling out offenders cause fear, shame, and feelings of violation. If a child is disruptive, speak to that child in private to get at the root of the problem. Keep your voice down—the louder you speak, the louder your children's voices tend to become.
- *Use eye contact* as a way to manage behavior. A long, searching gaze, a quick glance of approval, eyes crinkled in amusement or widened in amazement can have a powerful effect on the mood in your space.
- *Anticipate problems* and adjust for them. (Remember your motto: "prepare and prevent"!) Give Tony the talker a hands-on role; seat Diana the dreamer away from the window, separate chatty best friends.
- *Arrive early.* Organize details and materials ahead of time so that you can be there to greet everyone by name and with a smile. A hurried teacher who arrives when kids are already gathered in the room waiting for things to happen is a teacher with two strikes against her.
- *Expect the best.* Rejoice over good behavior. Catch kids being good and reinforce that behavior.

It's what Jesus would do!

19
Living with Labels

Have you encountered the alphabet soup of labels that are attached to kids these days? Medical professionals use over 100 labels and acronyms to identify learning disabilities in kids! In fact, it's quite likely that one label or another from their list has been attached to a child in your classroom. Unless you're living in Shangri-la, it's almost certain that a child in your neighborhood, a child in your church family, and a child in your own group has some disability that affects his or her learning and behavior. (Conservative estimates say one in ten people has a disability that affects capacity to learn and/or behavior.)

This brief chapter can't begin to cover the "disability" picture, but it will help you understand the challenge of dealing with a "labeled" child and offer suggestions you may be able to incorporate in your teaching. (For more detailed information about learning disabilities, check out these resources from Faith Alive: *Learning Disabilities and the Church* by Cynthia Holder Rich and Martha Ross-Mockaitis (2006), *Autism and Your Church* by Barbara J. Newman (2006), and *Helping Kids Include Kids with Disabilities* by Barbara J. Newman (2001).

Children who are born with learning or attention deficit disabilities, or who acquire them through accidents or illness, "may have difficulty reading, writing, responding, listening, sitting still, and behaving appropriately in traditional worship and Sunday school settings" say Rich and Mockaitis. "Such individuals can present a real challenge—and opportunity—for congregational ministries."

Right! So how can we meet the challenge and make the most of these opportunities?

First, it is important to examine our attitudes. Disruptive children are difficult to have in the classroom. (Some teachers have even said, "Either that child goes, or I do.") It's an understandable reaction, especially when one child upsets an entire roomful of children, making it impossible for everyone to have a great learning experience.

But if we examine our hearts, we know that's not what Jesus would do. Jesus championed those who were excluded, who were difficult, who hovered on the periphery of society. He said "Let the children come to me," and he didn't mean just the compliant, easy-to-handle kids. If you have a child with a disability in your classroom, remember that God loves him very much and wants him to experience that love. There are better ways than exclusion to solve disruptive behavior.

Second, it's essential to remember that kids with labels are much more than their labels! Most children with learning disabilities and those who have attention deficit disorders are of average or greater intelligence; they often have special gifts to contribute to the rest of the group. They may see things from a unique perspective, which can enhance everyone's learning. God has made them a part of your classroom community, and they have a significant place in it. No one may say, "We don't need you."

So how exactly can you deal with children who may disrupt the calm of your classroom community? Besides those suggestions noted in chapters 17 and 18, consider the following:

- *Ask an adult or teen-aged "friend" to join your group* to help keep a child with behavior issues on track. Such a child often finds it hard to focus and is highly distractible. Having someone sit beside her to help her focus and to curb her impulsive reactions will go a long way toward making the situation better for everyone. A special friend will also minimize the difficulties such kids have with a changing roster of teachers—at least *one* person will be a constant from week to week.
- *Consult with parents.* Many parents of kids diagnosed with special learning or behavioral needs are already very involved in their child's education. They've probably consulted with experts and developed their own strategies for dealing with these issues. Approach parents lovingly; they may be emotionally fragile as a result of their children's ongoing needs. (For example, you might say, "I've noticed Bonnie has a hard time sitting still. Can you give me some ideas on how to handle this?" rather than, "Boy, your kid is hyper!")
- *Model acceptance.* Many kids with learning disabilities find themselves low on the social ladder and are easy targets for taunts or teasing, which only lowers their already fragile self-esteem. Your love and acceptance, along with your open support for these children, will model for the rest of the group how to be inclusive and caring.
- *Be aware of the following areas* that may create particular difficulty for kids in your group who have learning or attention differences:

Transitions (moving from one activity to the next): Some kids with learning disabilities focus or fixate on one thing and have a hard time moving on. Give ample notice before moving the group to the next activity.

Distractions (cluttered walls and music playing in the background, for example): Children with learning disabilities benefit from pared-down surroundings. Is it possible to create a small space in your room that's free of distractions where they can work on their own?

Remembering things: Help children remember what you teach them—review material from the previous session before moving on to new material. Review rules often. When giving instructions, break them into small pieces and ask everyone to repeat them after you.

Sitting still: Some children need permission to stand or move around, perhaps at the back of the room to minimize distractions for others. Use stretch breaks and movement exercises frequently to minimize stress and increase attention.

Relationships: Impulsive or compulsive behavior may alienate peers. Children with behavior issues need to know that their socially unacceptable behavior has consequences—time-outs, apologizing, making it up to the person they've hurt. Sometimes it takes kids with learning disabilities longer to "warm up" to teachers too. If you're sharing the job with other teachers or aren't there every week, try to find ways to bring consistency for such kids (having a special adult or teen friend for the child works well).

- *Provide routine and structure* to benefit the children in your group who need it most. Rituals are helpful, as is consistently enforcing rules so kids know what to expect. Inform parents if any changes in programming are about to happen so they can help prepare their child.
- *Plan teaching activities that use a variety of senses.* Some children, especially those with learning disabilities, aren't as able to process information presented verbally or in written form. (It's like trying to understand someone speaking or writing in Greek!) Using visual cues, body movement, music, and other tactile devices may help these kids learn more effectively.

- *Think positive.* If you're looking for the negative, you're going to find it; but the reverse is also true. Reinforce the gifts of each child, and appreciate each as a child of God. Encourage kids to suggest their own solutions for their problems and to advocate for themselves. Give them permission to ask for help when they need it. Your positive attitude towards kids' learning and progress will reduce the stress they're feeling and give them confidence.

20 Being Well, Being Safe

It might be hard to listen to stories about Jesus, the Bread of Life, if you're feeling hungry for a piece of toast. And stories about how Jesus protects us from danger won't make a big impact if you're terrified by the bully in the church hallway.

Yes, children need Jesus—but it's hard for kids to meet and know Jesus if their other needs are not being met first. Psychologist Abraham Maslow developed a hierarchy of needs (see chart on page 63), suggesting that some needs people have take precedence over others. Basic physiological needs (for food, air, and water) as well as safety needs (for security and freedom from fear) must be satisfied before people will seek to satisfy higher needs such as the need for love, self-esteem, and achievement—and the need for spiritual growth.

What does that mean for you as a leader? It means that you must first be sensitive to your children's physical needs and also ensure that their need for safety and security is satisfied as you move on to focus on their higher needs.

Physical needs: Hungry children are listless learners who can't concentrate. Take action if some children in your group come to class hungry.

- If you suspect a child's family is having financial difficulties, get your deacons involved. This isn't just your problem; it's a situation that belongs to the whole church family.
- If families seem too rushed on Sunday mornings for breakfast, think of a creative solution. Can you tactfully ask parents to remedy the situation? Or perhaps you can invite children to think of ways to solve this problem themselves.
- Young children and children going through growth spurts digest food quickly. You may want to consider having a nutritious snack as a part of every session.

Safety needs: These include the need for security and stability; protection from harm; freedom from fear, anxiety, and chaos; and the need for structure, order, law, and limits.

- Make sure your church enforces a child safety policy. Such policies include procedures for screening teachers and helpers, for accompanying children to the bathroom, physical standards for furniture and toys, and other protections for children. (For more information, see *Preventing Child Abuse: Creating a Safe Place*, Faith Alive Christian Resources; see also chapters 26 and 27.)
- If you become aware that a child in your group is being abused in some way, you must, by law, report that abuse to your supervisors, and if need be, to community authorities.
- Gear your rules toward children's physical and emotional wellbeing and safety—and enforce them consistently.
- Anticipate possible problems to prevent them from happening. Ask what could possibly go wrong. Setting limits and giving specific instructions will prevent lots of accidents.
- Your attitude of acceptance and care, and your zero tolerance of bullying, ridicule, and harassment will create an environment that's free of anxiety and fear.

In all of this, you are following Jesus' lead. He fed the crowds when they were hungry and calmed the stormy seas when his disciples were afraid. He reprimanded the Pharisees when they became abusive and protected the woman caught in an act of adultery. Then Jesus offered his love, his forgiveness, and his Spirit to dwell within us so that we may become all that he means us to be!

That's what we're called to for the children in our care.

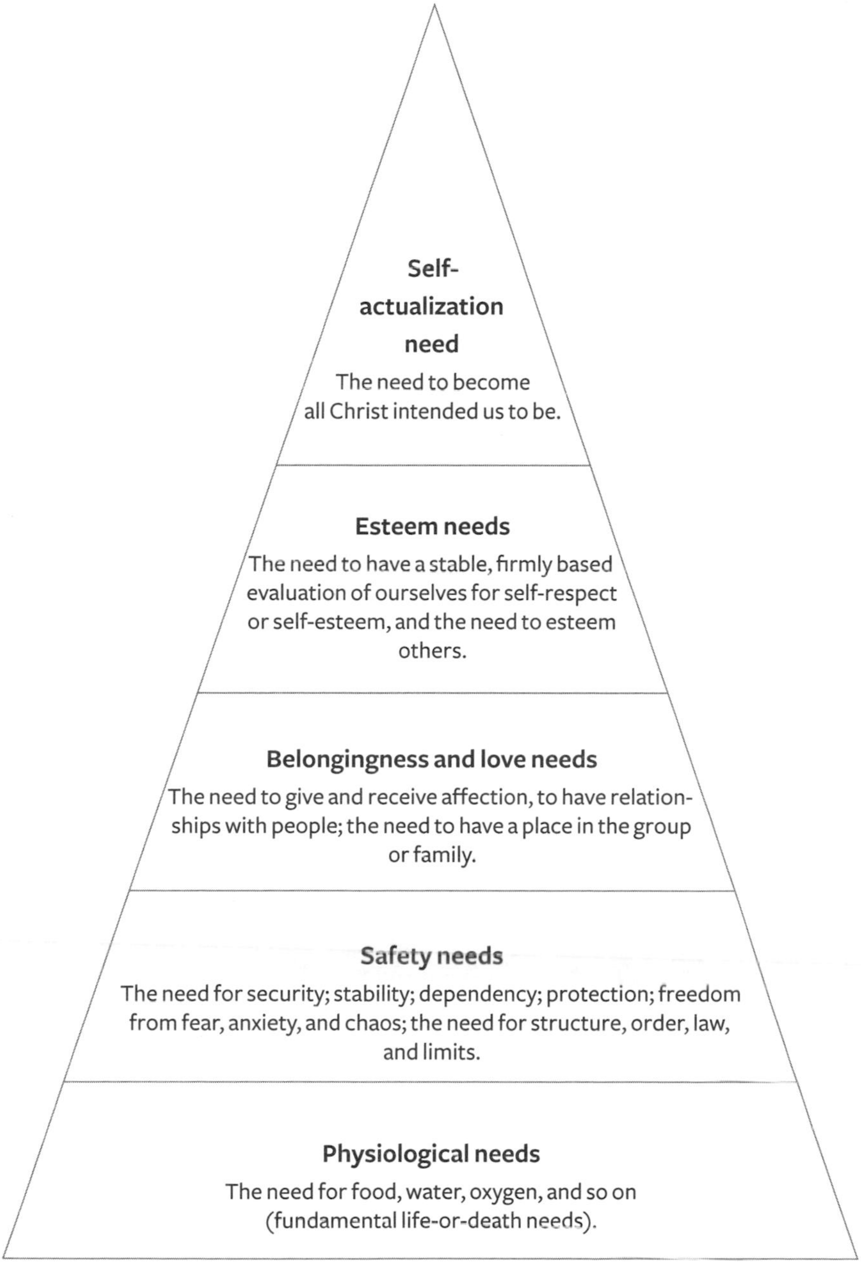
Self-actualization need
The need to become all Christ intended us to be.
Esteem needs
The need to have a stable, firmly based evaluation of ourselves for self-respect or self-esteem, and the need to esteem others.
Belongingness and love needs
The need to give and receive affection, to have relationships with people; the need to have a place in the group or family.
Safety needs
The need for security; stability; dependency; protection; freedom from fear, anxiety, and chaos; the need for structure, order, law, and limits.
Physiological needs
The need for food, water, oxygen, and so on (fundamental life-or-death needs).

Maslow's Hierarchy of Needs

21 Talk to Me!

What do kids do best? Talk and move! Yet what do teachers often want them to do? Be quiet and sit still. What's wrong with this picture?

A study by educator Dr. Ned Flanders indicates that talk by teachers in classrooms comprises 70-90 per cent of classroom interaction. Perhaps in a typical Sunday school class the percentages are a little better, but it's likely still true that children generally feel discouraged from talking to you or to each other.

What's the value of kids talking? Learning is a social process—it involves checking out your own understanding against what others perceive. Learning is also an active process that involves conversation, questions, rephrasing for clarification, discussion, and argument. Talking things through helps children identify gaps in their own knowledge and acquire new information.

Growth and change occur when children actively participate in the learning process. And that means *talking*—lots of it. When a teacher does all the talking, the only things that may be growing are the teacher's ego and the kids' apathy.

A Chinese proverb says, "I hear and I forget. I see and I remember. I do and I understand." Psychologists say that's true. We only retain up to 10 percent of what we hear; adding visual aids may boost our retention to 50 percent. But add *doing* to the mix (talking, discussions, role-playing) and the retention rate rises to 90 percent! Says Christian educator Howard Hendricks, "Unfortunately the bulk of Christian education is hearing oriented. That's why it's often so inefficient."

Your room provides kids with a perfect setting for talking things through with you, their teacher. You can encourage children to ask questions, voice any confusion, and express their doubts and fears. (Check out the next chapter, "Listen Up!" for ways to respond.)

It's important to keep everyone focused and talking about the right things. *Dwell* includes a variety of activities that appeal to multiple intelligences and that direct children to explore the meaning of the story each week. You'll find ideas like the following throughout the material:

- Pair and share: Ask a question and then have kids discuss it in pairs.
- Introduce a talking circle/talking stick: Gather children in a circle, sitting on the floor. Ask a question and pass a "talking stick" to someone who wants to contribute. Whoever has the talking stick gets to speak. The talking stick goes around and across the circle as children volunteer to contribute their ideas.
- Involve the group in brainstorming.
- Have kids retell the Bible story to the whole group or in small groups.
- Invite kids to answer each other's questions.
- Set up debates.
- Invite children to share stories about their week and make prayer requests
- Have kids respond to wondering questions.
- Have a child teach part of a session (or lead the singing, pray, read the Bible story).
- Invite children to interview each other, or you, or a special guest.

Your classroom may be noisier when children are encouraged to talk, but noise is often the sound of increased involvement, learning, and the joy of discovery. "Where did we get the idea that God loves 'shhh' and 'drab' and 'anything will do'?" asks poet and Presbyterian elder Ann Weems. "I think it's blasphemy not to bring our joy into his church." (from *Balloons Belong in Church* by Ann Weems, quoted by Marlene D. LeFever in *Creative Teaching Methods*, Cook Ministry Resources, 1985.)

Amen!

22
Listen Up!

God made people with two ears and only one mouth. As we learned in chapter 21, however, teachers tend to talk much more than they listen.

One of the most precious gifts you can give to the children in your group is to truly listen to them. When you listen to a child, you're telling her (no words needed!) that she's important. When you listen, you are also modeling God's gracious listening ears, showing kids that God listens to them too. When you listen, really listen to children, you're giving them permission, inviting them to ask important questions and explore their faith.

But listening involves more than ears—it also involves the heart, the mind, and the will. In a *Family Circus* cartoon, the little girl is tugging at her daddy's sleeve as he's buried in the newspaper. "Daddy," she insists, "you need to listen to me with your eyes as well as your ears."

Listening does not come naturally to most of us. But it's a skill that can be learned. Here are some tips for active listening:

- *Listen with your whole body.* Maintain eye contact. Gesture, nod, smile, lean into the conversation. Do whatever you can to show children that you are engaged with them. Kids need to know that you're listening not only to their words but also to their hearts.
- *Watch for body language* that reflects more than what the child is saying. Only a small part of communication happens through words. Drooping shoulders and folded arms speak volumes. So do sparkling eyes and dancing toes.
- *Give children permission to talk.* Begin conversations with open-ended starters such as "Tell me about your day" or "I wonder how you feel about your sick dog." Often children need to be encouraged to talk, to know that you are really interested.
- *Don't interrupt!* Listening takes patience. Children have a more limited vocabulary and take longer to express themselves than adults. Inviting them to share their concerns makes them vulnerable; an interruption may squash that hesitant attempt to express and share a thought or idea.

- *Wait to formulate your response* until the child is finished talking. Children can read eyes and body language very quickly—they'll know if you've jumped to conclusions before they're finished explaining themselves.
- *Ask further questions* for clarification if you're not sure you're hearing the essence of what a child is saying. Rephrase what you think you're hearing, then ask, "Is this what you're saying, or am I getting it wrong?"
- *Reflect children's feelings back to them.* Often kids can't name their feelings with words or are afraid to name them. You can help by articulating them. Saying, "It sounds like you're sad that your friend has found a new buddy to hang out with" may bring relief that an unspoken feeling has been validated.
- *Ask for children's opinions* regularly. (They definitely have them!) Ask them how they feel about war and what they think is the most important problem world leaders need to address. Asking for kids' opinions communicates respect for their ideas. Accept opinions that are expressed without challenging their rightness. You may want to ask follow-up questions to help the child think through implications, but a child's opinion is a child's opinion. Let it be!
- *Share your own questions* and uncertainties (subject to age-appropriate discernment, of course). For instance, say something like "I'd really like to redecorate our classroom walls, but I don't know where to begin. Any ideas?"
- *Extend conversations by asking good questions* that reveal more about the child's world. Children are usually eager to talk about themselves and their lives, from the mundane to the sublime. You have a great opportunity to learn more about kid culture and about the children themselves.

When adults model good listening, children learn essential communication skills. The greatest audience a child can have is a caring, thoughtful, interested adult who is important to them. That's you!

23 Using Symbols and Rituals

Kids love symbols. (That's why *Dwell* makes such a big deal of the story symbols you'll find throughout the curriculum!) If you doubt the importance of symbols, check out popular items marketed for children, all containing identifiable brand markings—symbols! Whether its Superman pjs, SpongeBob backpacks, or Dora the Explorer sneakers, brands mark the wearer as part of the "in" group. Rituals often serve the same purpose, helping children identify with a certain crowd of kids or a particular way of life.

Rituals and symbols are part of a long Christian tradition. God himself instituted the Passover and other annual feasts and festivals to remind people of his goodness. The rocks piled up after crossing the Jordan and the furnishings of the temple had symbolic and ritual significance. The first Christians wore the fish symbol as a secret message to others of their affiliation. And the church today often uses such visual cues as the cross, the dove, and liturgical colors to help Christians remember important themes of their faith.

Using signs or symbols and celebrating rituals helps children sense their connection to a very long line of believers as they learn the language of the church and of their faith; they'll realize they are bound to others in the family of God with cords that cannot be broken.

Repeated rituals and the use of symbols are incorporated into *Dwell* session plans. As a teacher, you'll also want to establish your own ceremonies and signs that draw your group together. Develop your own ways of using the story symbols; create a name and "coat of arms" that represents your group; begin each session with the same call and response or the same song; establish a special greeting such as a high-five; develop a special ritual for entering a time of reflection on the story—all of these are ways to build community.

Here are some more ideas for using symbol and ritual, taken from the book *Sign and Symbol, Word and Song* by Amy Florian (Ave Maria Press, Inc. 2001). Include some or all of the following *symbols* as standard parts of your meeting space:

- *A Bible*, preferably on its own table, attractively highlighted with a cloth or flowers.

- *A transparent pitcher and bowl filled with water* as a symbol of baptism and forgiveness; a small jug of oil (olive oil scented with vanilla) as a symbol of healing. Use oil in rituals of blessing each other or in prayers for healing.
- *Candles:* Have candles in different colors for the liturgical seasons to light at the beginning of each session or before prayer time.
- *Flowers and plants*, symbols of life and growth. You might want to plant seeds or cuttings the first Sunday of a class year and watch them grow throughout the year.
- *Banners or other art forms* that depict common symbols—wheat, grapes, chalice, dove.

Incorporate *rituals* such as the following into every session:

- *Begin class with a two- to five-minute ritual* (such as a blessing, passing the peace, responsive reading, lighting a candle to indicate a moment of silent prayer). This calms children, creates an atmosphere of prayer and reverence, and draws them into a shared faith experience. When celebrating a ritual, become a participant and invite children to take turns leading it.
- *Model ritual postures and gestures*, and invite children to imitate you: extending arms to the sides and lifting hands (the orans position) to indicate prayer; touching the head, lips, and chest after listening to Scripture to indicate that God's Word is present in our minds, words, and heart; using processions, perhaps with banners and percussion instruments, to lead to a prayer corner; standing proud and tall when the Bible is being read, kneeling when praying; extending the hand in blessing to another person or holding hands in a circle; passing a blessing around the circle; laying on of hands (on shoulder or top of head) when praying for a child's specific need.
- *Establish rituals to celebrate special occasions* such the beginning or ending of a church school year and children's birthdays. For instance, you could measure the children's height at the beginning and end of a year to indicate growth, reminding children that they grow not only physically but also spiritually. Or have children take a pledge of commitment and sign a book at the beginning of a unit or a new year.

Enjoy using symbol and ritual with the kids in your group. Not only will their learning be enhanced, but your group will become a closer community of faith.

24 The Fine Art of Storytelling

Author Elie Wiesel writes, "God made man because he loves stories." Perhaps there's truth in that wonderful statement. I suppose God could have proclaimed the gospel message in twenty-five words or less: "I made you to live in relationship with me. You sinned and broke that relationship. I sent my son Jesus to redeem you." Instead, God gave us the Bible, a book that proclaims God's love and faithfulness—story after story.

When you agreed to teach kids, you accepted God's command to keep telling these stories. And telling them *well* is important! Jim Rayburn, founder of Young Life, says, "It's a sin to bore a kid with the gospel." God's stories are *not* boring—they're alive, exciting, and possess the power of a two-edged sword. "Boring Bible storyteller" should be an oxymoron.

Dwell is all about God's story, as you can see by a quick glance at the names of the session steps: Gathering for God's Story, Entering the Story, Living into the Story, and Living Out of the Story. Your role as teacher is to become chief storyteller—and to invite your kids to retell the story and reflect on it each week so that it becomes *their story*.

> Look for opportunities in addition to the Bible story presentation to tell kids other good stories: stories about people who have done great and small things in God's kingdom, stories from your own life that illustrate a session truth, stories about other people who've experienced God's grace. Good preparation and thoughtfulness can transform a ho-hum story into one that sticks in children's minds and hearts for a long time.

Here are some suggestions for telling stories well:

Prepare well

Get your facts straight. Go straight to the source—read the story from the Bible. Read through the passage several times, perhaps in different versions. Then read the background reflection ("Getting into the Story") in your leader's guide.

As part of your preparation, identify the four parts of the story you'll be telling. For example, the four parts of Jesus' story of the Good Samaritan are

1. *Beginning:* a short, direct introduction ("There was a man who traveled from Jerusalem to Jericho . . . ")
2. *Action:* a recounting of what's happening, the problem to be solved, the resolution ("He was attacked . . . along came a priest . . . ")
3. *Climax:* the high point of the resolution: ("The Samaritan bandaged the traveler's wounds . . .")
4. *Ending:* the wrap-up, short and to the point. ("The Good Samaritan departed, leaving money, asking for nothing in return.")

Conclude your preparation by practicing telling the story in front of a mirror or a sympathetic audience—or record your telling. Practice is especially important for beginning storytellers. Practice will give you confidence and fix the story in your mind. If you're using visual aids or props, incorporate them into your practice session. If you depend on a script, look for a way to incorporate it into your props (for example, a king going into battle might be carrying a shield to which you can attach the script).

Tell it well

Here are some ways to enhance your effectiveness:

- Dress simply. Avoid flashy jewelry, clothing, or scents that might distract your listeners.
- Use your voice as an instrument. Vary the pitch (high to low), the volume (soft to loud), the speed (slow to fast), the intensity (flat, excited, sad, worried) of your voice.
- Keep props and visual aids simple. Kids have wonderful imaginations—a pair of sandals and a walking stick will give them raw material to imagine a story's character and setting. Elaborate props may distract from the story itself.
- Communicate with your body in addition to your words. Use your hands, eyes, shoulders, and your whole body to enhance the story's message; but again, keep it simple.
- Use cue cards to help if you're worried about losing track of the story. Write key words, phrases, or sentences on cards and arrange them in sequence. (Use them only when necessary.)

- *Let the story stand on its own feet.* Don't add moralisms, meanings, or conclusions. Children will wonder about and ponder God's story, and the Holy Spirit will help them come to their own conclusions.

In one African culture, a ritual chant signals the beginning of a story. "A story! A story!" says the storyteller, announcing his intention. "Let it come! Let it come!" respond the eager listeners.

God's story . . . let it come! The Holy Spirit will do the rest.

Check out *The Creative Storytelling Guide for Children's Ministry* by Steven James (Standard Publishing, 2002) for many more ideas and examples of different ways to tell a story well.

25 Living God's Story

With the basics of storytelling in place, it's time to look at how you would use these techniques effectively to help your kids enter and live into God's big story as it's presented in *Dwell*.

In Step 2 of each session (Entering the Story) you'll generally be preparing to tell the story yourself or present it as a drama. Here's some advice that will make this important step a bit easier for you:

- Be sure to *get drama scripts to other presenters as early as possible*, preferably a week or more in advance so participants can prepare. Make it easy for readers by highlighting each part in a bright color.
- *If you're inviting a guest storyteller to present the Bible story to the group, offer a brief summary of the unit theme and content*, explain what's come before and will come after this particular story, and mention any situations or issues the storyteller should be aware of (for example, your group uses a ritual chant for quieting down just before the story). The more your guest storyteller knows, the easier it will be to establish rapport with the kids.
- Often scripts call for audience volunteers. *Keep a list of good readers and natural actors to call on* when there are substantive roles. Offer less gifted readers and younger participants roles that involve pantomime, sound effects, or moving props around. In this way you'll use everyone's gifts while ensuring the best story presentation possible.
- Anything that can go wrong will go wrong. So *be prepared and remain flexible*. When the flashlight you're using as a key prop runs out of juice at just the wrong time, what will you do? If a key participant doesn't make it to church, is there someone to pinch hit?
- *The details count*—big time. Can everybody see the storyteller(s)? (If there's a window behind them, kids may only be seeing their silhouettes!) Can everyone hear the story? (Perhaps you need to present the story in a smaller space or invest in a sound system.) Are kids seated comfortably? Is there enough space so they can stretch out their arms for motions? Is the room temperature comfortable? (A

room that's too warm will make children restless; too cold and they'll be distracted from listening.) Would the group benefit from a ritual to settle them down for listening?

- If you're not a part of the story presentation yourself, be sure to *take your place in the audience along with the kids*. By doing so, you are modeling good story-listening behavior. The kids are watching you—if you are at the back of the room doing other things, they'll notice. Be an eager and involved listener!

> Even if you're not a direct participant in the story presentation, it's important to ground yourself in the goals and central truth of the session and how the story fits into the theme of the unit you're teaching. Preparing gives you the confidence to focus the children's learning on the story and your goals for the session.

Steps 3 and 4 of each session (Living into the Story and Living Out of the Story) invite children to make each story their own. Here are some ways to help kids interact with the story effectively:

- *Make connections*. Each session presents only a part of God's *whole* story. How does this story fit into God's big story? How does it flow with the theme of your unit? As you live into the story for the day, remind children of the stories they've been listening to in past weeks and help them find the links.
- *Take time to review*. The story presented in Step 2 is just that—a presentation. What follows in Steps 3 and 4 is an opportunity to make sure that kids caught the details and understood the action (especially God's action!). Take time to ask factual and wondering questions, and if need be, to revisit story details.
- *Invite participation*. Make sure the children have ample time to process the story they've reenacted. Give them opportunities to ask questions, to ponder, to wonder. Remember the people who first listened to Jesus' stories; though often they did not understand what Jesus was telling them, they carried his parables away and pondered them. Perhaps later in the day it dawned on them—"Aha! So that's what he meant!" That's the kind of wondering you'll want to encourage.
- *Encourage commitment too!* That's what "Living Out of the Story" is all about. Jesus said that bearing fruit is the natural outcome of

being connected to him. Nudge children to go beyond pondering and reflecting to acting and living out of God's story.

> "There's a saying in the Jewish tradition that the shortest distance between [a hu]man and God is through a story. So if storytelling is a journey, sacred storytelling is a pilgrimage—a pilgrimage to a place called Hope." —Andy Fraenkel

26 Preventing Abuse

Jesus said, "When you receive the childlike on my account, it's the same as receiving me. But if you give them a hard time, bullying or taking advantage of their simple trust, you'll soon wish you hadn't. You'd be better off dropped in the middle of the lake with a millstone around your neck" (Matthew 18:5-7, *The Message*). Harsh words about a harsh issue.

Jesus took the faith nurture of children very seriously. As we've learned, feeling safe and secure is a basic human *need*, and when children are subjected to physical, sexual, or emotional abuse, we've deprived them of that safety and security. What's more, the love and security significant adults give children form the foundation of their understanding of God's love. So suffering abuse at the hands of caregivers and church workers strikes a heavy blow to the emotional and faith development children.

What constitutes abuse? The Hospital for Sick Children in Toronto defines it this way: "Child abuse is any kind of harm to a child's body, emotional pain, neglect, or use for sexual purposes that can cause injury or psychological damage to a child." Hitting, bullying, criticism, exploitive touching, and ignoring a child can all be forms of abuse. Your church, like many others, may have instituted an abuse policy that safeguards the children in its ministries and programs. If so, be sure to read and follow it carefully. If not, approach your church leaders about instituting such guidelines. A typical abuse policy includes such things as

- *Screening and training:* Churches may require every program volunteer to undergo a criminal background check. They may also insist that volunteers receive training and sign an agreement to abide by their policy. It's helpful to know that these policies protect not only the children from abuse but the volunteers from false allegations of abuse.
- *Reporting:* If you do become aware of possible abuse committed either by church workers or the caregivers of a child in your group, it's your moral obligation to protect that child from further abuse by reporting what you know to civil or church authorities.

- *Reducing the risks:* One-to-one contact between a staff person/volunteer and a child increases the probability of an incident or allegation, so most abuse policies offer clear guidelines, such as having two volunteers or staff present at every session; asking permission of a parent if you do need to meet a child alone, and meeting in a public place; having hall monitors on duty during program time so children will be safer when going to the bathroom and suspicious behavior will more likely be observed.
- *Safe and healthy touching:* Humans thrive when they receive physical displays of affection, like touching. Unfortunately, rules are necessary for protecting children and leaders alike. When it comes to touching a child, holding hands, side-by-side hugs (the "A-frame hug"), and a hand on the shoulder are safer alternatives to frontal hugs or an arm around the waist. Never touch a child who seems to shy away from touches. And never, ever kiss a child.
- *Appropriate use of discipline:* Discipline becomes abuse when a child is blamed by an adult to justify the discipline that the adult administers; when it results in pain, injury, or humiliation to the child; when one child is singled out, even though others are also behaving unacceptably; or, when it is administered excessively over a short period of time.

Much of this information may seem to focus on the negative—"Don't do it!" Thankfully, there are many other behaviors to which you can say, "Yes! Do it!"

- Do respect children as imagebearers of God, worthy of love and dignity.
- Do all you can to protect kids' (and your own) dignity and reputation.
- Do cultivate the fruit of the spirit: "love, joy, peace, patience, kindness, goodness, faithfulness, gentleness and self-control. Against such things there is no law" (Gal. 5:22-23).

27

Creating a "No-Bully Zone"

Bullying. Just say the word, and most people have a story to tell.

Bullying always leaves its mark. For some that mark may be small and insignificant, but for others it can be a huge scar that twists the psyche. Bullying is a form of abuse that has received considerable attention lately, and it's an important issue for *Dwell* leaders. When churches and their ministry leaders ignore this problem because they're convinced that bullying doesn't happen in Christian communities, they're hiding their heads in the sand. Bullying happens *everywhere* children gather.

Bullying and its effects will hamper your efforts to build community with God, with fellow learners and leaders, and with families. It is neither a normal "rite of passage" nor a challenge that will make kids stronger (or "tougher") in the end. Repeated incidents often become pivotal memories in the faith journeys of bullied children. The results can be especially harmful when such behavior happens in church.

Although adults in charge of children's programs believe they intervene and resolve most incidents of bullying, kids beg to differ. In one study, 70 percent of teachers but only 25 percent of students said adults "almost always" intervene to stop bullying ("Bullying at School," *Education Canada*). Children are generally afraid to report bullying because they believe they shouldn't be "ratting" on their classmates. Instead they often withdraw from the unhappy situation. It's possible that some kids who have quit coming to your program have dropped out for this reason.

So what can you do to ensure that bullying doesn't happen on your watch? Here are some pointers gathered from organizations that have studied the issue of bullying and its effects on kids:

Prevention:

- Create a climate of openness: talk openly about bullying; tell children that you will listen and take action if they tell you about instances of bullying.
- Enlist children's cooperation in putting together a list of rules to make your classroom a "no-bully zone."

- Ensure that there is always adequate supervision in hallways, restrooms, and other places where children gather.

Creating a healing environment:

- Bullies need to be held accountable. Follow the three R's: *Restitution* (paying for a broken toy, giving back extorted money, apologizing for malicious words); *Resolution* (figuring out a way to keep it from happening again such as counting to ten when the child is angry, or recognizing the stimulus that causes the bullying behavior and deciding on a better coping mechanism); *Reconciliation*: (finding a way to heal the broken relationship).
- Check out any resources your church offers that can help hurt kids recover; bullied children need a place to tell their stories and help in putting the incidents behind them. Bullies need healing too. Often these children are victims themselves, and have been taught poor ways of relating to others.

Nurturing empathy:

Studies show that empathy is the antidote to bullying. When we begin to identify with poor, hurting, and disadvantaged people, we learn healthy, Christ-like ways of relating that bring hope instead of fear. Here are ways to nurture empathy in your kids:

- Practice positive discipline: help bullies identify what they have done wrong and take ownership of the problem; help them develop a process for solving the problem while leaving their dignity intact.
- Spotlight feelings. Questions about feelings can be a part of every session; encourage children to imagine the feelings of Bible characters or to voice their own feelings about stories they hear or events they experience. Teachers and leaders should not feel as though they need to "fix" feelings as soon as they are expressed; allow children to be honest and help them work through to the positives.
- Role play is an excellent strategy that helps kids identify with the feelings and ideas of others. A word of caution: lead up to role plays by talking with the group, describing the scenario to be dramatized. (For example: "One of the characters in this role play has just been tripped in the hallway. What might he be thinking as he

gets up off the floor?") Once children are into imagining the scenario, assign roles and proceed.

- Encourage journaling or writing exercises that focus on another person's perspective: What did the little boy who gave his lunch to Jesus tell his mom when he came home?
- Teach about real-life people who model empathy, and how this empathy resulted in great things: Nelson Mandela, Mother Teresa, Martin Luther King, Jr.
- Plan service projects, especially hands-on work with people who are disabled or who live in poverty. Often bullies believe they are entitled to whatever they wish; working for others and learning about their lives often teaches new attitudes.
- Invite kids to practice empathic reactions: present a hypothetical situation a child might encounter (a friend's parents have divorced or a grandpa is dying). Ask questions like these: How is he or she feeling about it? What could I do in response?
- Praise positive behavior: watch for examples of kids being kind and loving to each other and reinforce that behavior!
- Provide opportunities for fellowship and friendship: parties, celebrations, projects, eating together, pen-pal relationships, and other activities offer warm and nurturing antidotes to negative experiences and may go a long way toward filling up empty places in a bully's life.

28 Praying with Children

In a letter to Jesus, Frankie, age eleven, wrote the following: "Please be with me on Thursday. I am running in a 3 mile race then. I will need all the speed in the world. If you are not busy with other things, maybe you could be at the starting line, the finish line, and everywhere in between" (from *Dear God: Children's Letters to God* by David Heller, Doubleday, 1987).

God loves to communicate with his children—young and old. If they talk, God listens. And if they listen, God will talk. And that's really what prayer is all about.

Are you looking for some ways to encourage the kids in your group to talk and listen to God? Here are some suggestions:

- Children learn by example. Do you pray? (Check out chapter 33 for ways to grow in your own prayer life.) It's pretty hard to teach kids something you do not practice yourself!
- Remember that child-like prayer is real prayer—your goal is not to teach children to pray adult prayers, complete with clichés, "holy" words, or pious expressions. Encourage children to come to God in their own way, to say what comes naturally in a simple, conversational way. Kids need to know that no one will laugh at their prayers or pronounce them "cute" or "sweet."
- Help children understand the purpose of prayer—it's the best way to build a relationship with God. Just as relationships grow when we talk often and openly to parents and friends, so we grow closer to God by talking regularly. And just as we talk to our families about a variety of things, our prayer conversations with God include praise, confession, thanks, and requests.
- Learn by doing: Involve children in different kinds of prayer as you approach God together:

    - "popcorn prayers": short, spontaneous, sentence prayers
    - prayer journals in which kids can write or draw their prayers
    - prayer walks: a walk through the community or church building with stops along the way to pray for specific needs and people

- prayer songs: graces, blessings, the Lord's Prayer, psalms put to music
- silence: opportunities for everyone to listen for the still, small voice within, or prepare their hearts and minds to meet God
- prayer request boards: displaying requests and answers to prayer in a public place
- prayer circles with a candle: a votive candle is passed around the circle, with each child holding the candle and praying aloud or silently.
- unison prayers: memorized prayers such as the Lord's Prayer

- Teach children prayer methods they can do on their own at home. The ACTS acrostic is a common one (Adoration, Confession, Thanksgiving, and Supplication). Or consider teaching them the Hand Prayer:

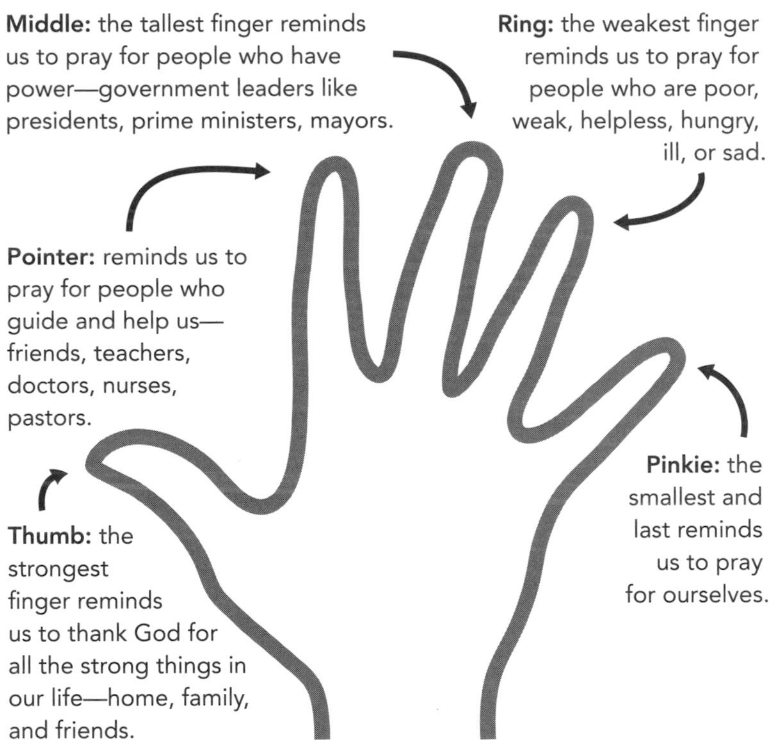
Middle: the tallest finger reminds us to pray for people who have power—government leaders like presidents, prime ministers, mayors.
Ring: the weakest finger reminds us to pray for people who are poor, weak, helpless, hungry, ill, or sad.
Pointer: reminds us to pray for people who guide and help us—friends, teachers, doctors, nurses, pastors.
Pinkie: the smallest and last reminds us to pray for ourselves.
Thumb: the strongest finger reminds us to thank God for all the strong things in our life—home, family, and friends.

For more ideas for ways to pray together, check out *The Praying Church Sourcebook* and *The Praying Church Idea Book*, both available from Faith Alive Christian Resources.

29

Taking Stock

You're still reading this book! You're in touch with kids and the world they inhabit, and you have a list of teaching strategies that might work. So what else do you need in order to be a vital part of the children's ministry in your church? This chapter offers an inventory for looking inward and keeping your heart in the right place as you lead God's kids. It's easy to become discouraged, even burned out, when you wonder deep down in your heart whether you are making a difference in kids' lives.

Teachers shouldn't have to take quizzes, but try this one out for size—it's actually more like an unofficial, nonscientific checklist to help you take a look at yourself. It focuses on three areas and will help you see where you shine—and where you might need a little polishing.

Check the statements that describe you *most or all of the time*. Be honest, but be kind to yourself too. Nobody's perfect; nobody measures up all of the time. If you read a particular statement and think "I'm *trying* to do that!" give yourself the benefit of the doubt. When you've finished, tally up your scores for each category, and read on to discover your strengths and the areas that could use a bit more work.

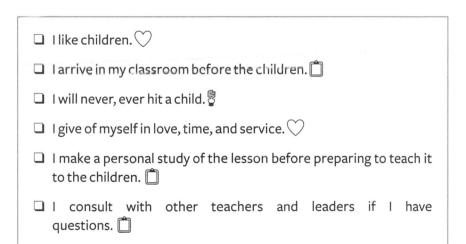

- ❑ I like children. ♡
- ❑ I arrive in my classroom before the children. 📋
- ❑ I will never, ever hit a child. 💡
- ❑ I give of myself in love, time, and service. ♡
- ❑ I make a personal study of the lesson before preparing to teach it to the children. 📋
- ❑ I consult with other teachers and leaders if I have questions. 📋

- ❑ I have regular times of Bible study and prayer so I can grow as a Christian. ♡
- ❑ I use language that is age-appropriate and explain unfamiliar words.
- ❑ I love Jesus, and I want to use the gifts he's given to me. ♡
- ❑ My heart's desire is to become all that Christ wants me to be. ♡
- ❑ I understand that I need to have a loving relationship with each child in my care. ♡
- ❑ I believe that there are reasons for misbehavior and I try to discover them.
- ❑ I begin preparation for teaching with prayer.
- ❑ I understand that children's attention spans are about one minute for each year (a five-year-old can focus for about five minutes on one activity).
- ❑ I evaluate the curriculum and adapt sessions to meet my group's needs.
- ❑ I treat children with as much love and respect as I do adults. ♡
- ❑ I am consistent in enforcing a few basic rules.
- ❑ I am sensitive to the needs of children and to what they are feeling and thinking. ♡
- ❑ I am aware of the materials available in the supply cupboard.
- ❑ I understand the concept of multiple intelligences and try to incorporate a variety of learning activities to reach every child.
- ❑ I make sure that there are adequate supplies to complete the activities.
- ❑ I speak to disruptive children privately to determine the root of the problem.

- ❏ I try to learn as much personal information about each child as possible.
- ❏ The children in my group know what I expect of them.
- ❏ I pray for the children in my group.
- ❏ I am aware of and use audiovisual resources available in my church.
- ❏ I lower my voice rather than raising it when addressing a noisy group.
- ❏ I try to see the world as a child sees it.
- ❏ I know who I can ask to substitute for me in an emergency situation.
- ❏ I believe it's just as important to rejoice over good behavior as it is to discipline misbehaviors.

Tally:

____ hearts ____ clipboards ____ light bulbs

Heart statements assess your commitment to ministry to children. If you checked fewer than six, you might ask yourself if you really want to teach kids. Children store up impressions and feelings in Sunday school that help form their emerging faith. As a *Dwell* leader, you teach by who you are—including your attitudes, casual words, expressions, and gestures. You are a model to your children!

Clipboard statements get at the important task of lesson preparation. If you checked fewer than six, you might be too busy! Teaching well requires time and effort outside of the classroom, not just inside it. Good preparation shows that you value your ministry to children and are willing to set aside the time to do it well . . . and reap the rewards.

Light bulb statements assess how familiar you are with techniques for good classroom management. If you checked fewer than six, take heart! These are skills you can learn by reading books, taking workshops, or observing experienced teachers.

If your heart's in the right place, if you're setting aside the time that's necessary to prepare, and if you're willing to learn, you're well on your way to being the kind of loving Sunday school teacher kids won't forget.

30
The Joy of Failure

There's not a lot to be said about failure except that it happens to everyone. Everyone. No exceptions.

Kids seem bored. Or they run all over you. The session you worked on so hard fell flat. Children challenge you with questions you can't answer. The unhappy child you've been praying for has dropped out of Sunday school. A feisty kid says flat-out that he doesn't believe in God anymore, and the rest of the kids seem to admire him. Sometimes teaching Sunday school feels like your "thorn in the flesh." Those are the times you can't help but wonder if you're really making a difference.

In his book *Help! I'm a Sunday School Teacher!* Ray Johnston offers some valuable advice: "Failure is never fatal—but discouragement can be! When I bomb (and it happens regularly), I find that two reminders keep me going. First, no teacher can connect with *every* kid. No Sunday school teacher is interesting every week. And no Sunday school teacher is liked by all the kids. You will have kids that are too cool, too flaky, or too bored—or they just won't like you. Give yourself a break. Chances are, if you are really honest, you don't like every kid either. Second, no kid is beyond God's reach. Have you thought about the disciples lately? Doubting Thomas, loud-mouthed Peter, and James and John always arguing over who was the greatest. Sound familiar? The next time you are ready to throw in the towel, remember the disciples and trust God to use you to reach your students in his timing" (Youth Specialties, 1995).

Truth is, there are *good* things about failure. Lots of good things. Here's a "top ten" list of things you gotta love about failure:

1. God loves people who fail just as much as people who succeed. God didn't give up on Moses, David, Jonah, Peter, and a host of other less-than-successful folks we meet in the Bible.
2. People who fail are people who are teachable. Problems and challenges get us down on our knees, talking to Jesus. And that, as Martha learned, is a good thing!

3. Failure leads to persistence. How many times did Thomas Edison invent the light bulb before he finally got a working model? Failure is not the end of the road, it's another step on the way to success.
4. Failure forces us to consult with others. Each of us is only one small part of Christ's body. Other people have gifts that will enrich us if we call on them for help. We'll grow in our appreciation for each other too.
5. Failure forces us to change our routine ways of doing things. If you keep doing things the same old way and it's not working, you need to try something else. Hurrah for learning new skills!
6. Failure teaches us reflective skills. The best way to avoid repeated failure is to figure out where we went wrong. This requires honesty and self-examination. And courage!
7. Learning from our failures will help us help others—we can speak from experience and others can benefit from our mistakes.
8. When we fail, we're in such good company. An African proverb says that a good cook has broken many pots. Famous leaders like Winston Churchill and Albert Einstein know from experience that failure is the natural outcome of learning and trying something new—in fact, first-time success is usually an aberration!
9. Failure forces us to face reality. Is what we are trying to accomplish workable? Do we need to change our goals or our methods? Do we need more resources or new strategies?
10. Failure teaches us to dream and to be creative. God will bless our efforts to honor him.

It's not all about you—or about me. It's all about God, who always knows what he is doing. Failure is an opportunity to live out something you really want your kids to learn—how to trust and obey our great God.

While you're at it, hang on to this promise:

> "As the rain and the snow come down from heaven, and do not return to it without watering the earth and making it bud and flourish, so that it yields seed for the sower and bread for the eater, so is my word that goes out from my mouth: It will not return to me empty, but will accomplish what I desire and achieve the purpose for which I sent it" (Isaiah 55:10-11).

31 Transparency—Use It!

Transparency isn't just another name for an "overhead"—it's also an essential quality of a good teacher. Transparent teachers are open and honest. They don't spend their energy trying to cover up or wear a mask that hides who they really are.

Genesis 3, the story of Satan's temptation of Adam and Eve, teaches us that the essence of evil is deceitfulness and lies. An adult who teaches children must never mislead the kids they've promised to teach. To do so may be to cause Jesus' "little ones," the ones he loved and died for, to stumble. Paradoxically, if you're not transparent, kids can see right through you!

To be true to Christ and to the kids you teach, cultivate honesty in your life.

- *Be honest with God.* God wants your commitment to him and to ministry among his people. Christians are people "on the way"—you don't have to be a perfect role model. Instead you're called to be a living, growing child of God, committed to letting God be the King of your life. Children of the King want to root out the sin that creeps into their hearts. If you've not yet submitted to God, confess your sin and ask for the Holy Spirit's help.
- *Be honest with yourself.* God knows that at times you will become tired, discouraged and ready to throw in the towel. You won't always feel "up" and full of excitement about your ministry to kids. Sometimes you won't even like them very much! Sometimes you'll wonder if you're the right person for this job. You needn't pretend to be a saint, tireless and ever eager to do good works. When you admit negative feelings to yourself, you're ready to take the next step—sharing them with God and with God's people. That's where you'll find the help you need. Being honest with yourself marks the beginning of growth and change.
- *Be honest with your fellow leaders.* Church leaders who organize children's programs are always looking for volunteers. You've said yes. And now it's up to you to let them know when you have questions,

problems, doubts, or frustrations. If you feel like you need more training, if the supplies you were promised don't materialize, if you feel like you need a little time off, speak up. Be honest. Don't hide issues that will fester and cause anger or discouragement.

- *Be honest with children.* No, you don't have to bare your soul and confess your darkest sins to your kids. But you should be able to say honestly that you are a sinner, that you have doubts or questions, that sometimes you struggle. If kids raise a question you can't answer, say so. If they catch you in an inconsistency, admit it. If something is troubling you—your mother's cancer, your spouse's unemployment, or your runaway dog—say so. When you become vulnerable, kids are more likely to come to you with their own problems. And who knows, they just might surprise you—by sending a card to your mother or praying for your spouse or making some posters to help you find your dog!

32 Rest Area Ahead

Perhaps you've noticed it on your favorite website: a little alert telling you that certain parts of the domain will be inaccessible for a while for maintenance. Without regular maintenance, things break down. That's why we take our cars in for an oil change. That's why we visit the dentist regularly. And that's why people who offer tune tune-ups, repairs, and renovations stay in business!

Without regular maintenance you might wear out too. Teaching is hard work. You need to balance your effort and energy with adequate time for rest. God says, "Catch your breath! Take a break. Come apart and be with me a while."

In his book *Rest*, Siang-Yang Tan describes four areas of our lives in which we need to experience rest: physical, emotional, relational, and spiritual. Busy people need to take care of their bodies, getting enough food, sleep, exercise, and leisure. We need to rest our minds so we can experience emotional peace, quiet, contentment, and serenity. We need to find relational harmony with others, including fellowship and deep friendships. Most of all, we need to find rest from guilt, doubt, and emptiness by living in faith from day to day.

It's a matter of obedience. God gave us a command—not a suggestion—to observe Sabbath rest. Sabbath is not a synonym for the pursuit of leisure or amusement, but rather a time of genuine refreshment for body, mind, and spirit. It is time when God's children rest from their work and drop their stresses at God's feet.

It's a matter of necessity. Scripture teaches that God created a rhythm in our lives—periods of work followed by times of rest. The same rhythm exists in creation: night leads to day, seasons unfold one after the other, tides flow in and out, plants become dormant only to burst into new life after a period of rest. God instituted the Sabbath, the year of Jubilee, and celebrations and festivals because he knew we needed times of rest in order to survive and grow. Rest is a necessity for those who give of themselves to others.

It's a matter of joy. Doing nothing gets a bad rap these days. For most people, action and accomplishment are far superior to inactivity or waiting. Our culture's anthem seems to be "Hurry, hurry, hurry—rush, rush, rush—more, more, more." And the result—which we see in increasing numbers of stress-related illnesses and psychological problems—is loss of joy. God has an antidote: Rest and recapture your joy. "You have made known to me the path of life; you will fill me with joy in your presence, with eternal pleasures at your right hand" (Psalm 116:11).

But how can I rest when there is so much work to do, you may wonder. Try this:

- *Follow Jesus' example.* He did not ask permission when he withdrew to a quiet place to pray. Although there were still people begging to be taught and healed and disciples to be led, Jesus spent time praying or having dinner with friends or fishing for the fun of it.
- *Set aside moments each day to take minibreaks.* A walk around the block can turn into a retreat if you ask God to walk with you. Be aware of God's presence beside you.
- *Simplify.* Our affluent and media-saturated world is filled with distractions that often waste our time and sap our energies. If it's not necessary, if it's not enriching your life, maybe it's time to get rid of it. Ask God to show you what's standing between you and rest in him.

Perhaps you have been teaching Sunday school for years and years and years without a break. Perhaps you are neglecting your own family to take care of the church's children. Perhaps your body, your emotions, your relationships, and your soul are suffering from want of rest. To you God says, "Take a break. I'm telling you, just do it. You need to rest. It will be good for you. Trust me."

33 Prayer Power

How important is prayer?

Christians from all times and places have been telling us that it's absolutely essential.

> *"Pray without ceasing."*
>
> —the apostle Paul

> *"Prayer is the mortar that holds our house together."*
>
> —Mother Teresa

> *"Prayer does not fit us for the greater work, prayer is the greater work."*
>
> —Oswald Chambers

> *"Prayer is the sum of our relationship with God. We are what we pray."*
>
> —Carlo Carretto

> *"Prayer does not change God, but it changes him who prays."*
>
> —Soren Kierkegaard

> *"I believe that true prayer makes us into what we imagine. To pray to God leads to becoming like God."*
>
> —Henri Nouwen

> *"You can do more than praying after you have prayed. You can never do more than praying before you have prayed."*
>
> —Corrie Ten Boom

> *"Seven days without prayer makes a person weak."*
>
> —Anonymous

Prayer is about growth and change. To pray is to be open to the Spirit of God working in you. And as you model Christ's love, growth is what you desire for yourself and for the children you teach.

How do busy people with lots of work to do find the time to pray? The secret is to pray as you *are*—not as you think you *ought*. There's no single "right" way to approach God. We all find ourselves in different life situations. The retired senior may find that a morning "quiet" time is the best way to pray, while a busy mom of three preschoolers can only pray as she wipes sticky hands and rocks babies to sleep. A businessman may turn a light-rail car into a prayer chapel as he uses his 50-minute commute to pray. A writer turns to the computer, a laborer kneels at the bedside each night, and an office worker keeps a small altar of stones on a filing cabinet as a reminder to pray for every client that comes through the door.

Besides having different life circumstances, we also have different personalities and qualities. (Multiple intelligences are a great example of this.) Some of us are reflective and some are active. Some pray best with words; others prefer to dance our praise. Some sing or paint their prayers, others keep an annotated prayer list.

If you are having difficulty sustaining a prayer life that nourishes your soul and connects you to God, perhaps you haven't found a way to pray that works for you. The following ideas come from various traditions and writings on prayer:

- *Let Scripture shape your prayer life.* Read a passage very slowly, several times, waiting to receive a word or phrase of instruction for your life. Write it down and reflect on it. How would you make this insight a daily part of your life? Pray, asking God's help and expressing gratitude for the gift of wisdom he's given to us in the Bible.
- *Pray the "Here I Am" prayer.* Find a comfortable and quiet place to sit undisturbed. Say, "Here I am, Lord. I will spend the next five minutes (*or however long you choose*) sitting quietly with you." Close your eyes and be aware of the sounds, the smells surrounding you. Listen to your breathing. Repeat the words "Here I am" whenever you find your attention wandering. Bask in God's presence.
- *Pray with music.* Choose a piece of music that has always moved you (it doesn't have to be "religious" music). Begin with silence, asking God to be present in the music. Listen to the piece several times, finding a phrase, a line, or a word that speaks especially to you. Reflect on

that selection, asking God to reveal what it has to say to your spiritual life. Speak (or write in a journal) to God about it.

- *Use the* "examen." This word means examination, and refers to the practice of checking out the best and most difficult parts of the day on a regular basis, perhaps in the evening before retiring. Review your day, asking yourself questions such as, When did I feel closest to God? When did I fail to reflect God's love? Give thanks for God's presence, and ask for God's mercy and forgiveness for those times you strayed. Resolve, with God's grace, to live out his purpose for your life, one day at a time.
- *Pray using beads or ribbons.* Create a visual reminder with beads or ribbons to help you pray. For instance, each bead in a string of five or ten could be a reminder of a certain issue or Scripture passage you wish to pray. Each ribbon in a braided bookmark could symbolize a specific person or need you wish to lift before God.
- *Practice the presence of God.* Centuries ago, Brother Lawrence wrote a classic book by this name. In it he described how he desired to be aware of God's presence beside him every moment of the day, and how he worked toward this goal. If this practice appeals to you, start by using the clock to remind yourself at specific, predetermined times, "God is here with me! Thank you, God!" Gradually, decrease the times between these reminders, until it becomes a natural habit to experience God's presence every moment of your day.
- *Pray on cue.* Use everyday situations in your life to remind you to pray. For instance, when you turn on the computer and hear its first beep, be reminded to pray for your workday. When you turn the key in your car's ignition, let it remind you to pray for traveling safety. Daily routines include lots of cues that can keep you connected to and dependent on God throughout your day.
- *Pray with your imagination.* Let your God-given imagination help you visualize those situations you want to lift before God. For example, if you are praying for healing for someone, create a mental image of that person in your imagination. Now focus on what needs healing, and present it, in your imagination, for God's safekeeping.
- *Create a wall of prayer.* Designate a special wall or door in your home as your prayer wall. Cover it with paper or posterboard (or use Post-It notes) to make a writing surface. Using different colored markers, draw or write praise and petitions you want to commit to God in prayer.

- *Pray with your whole self.* Rather than using just thoughts or words, express your prayers with motion. Begin with a prayer of intention, telling God that you offer your movement—walking, running, dancing—to him, and asking him for an open, receptive heart. Then proceed with your movement, listening, observing, and waiting for whatever God may choose to show you.

Remember, as Rick Warren points out in *The Purpose-Driven Life*, God "wants more than an appointment in your schedule. He wants to be included in *every* activity, every conversation, every problem, and even every thought. You can carry on a continuous open-ended conversation with him throughout your day, talking with him about whatever you are doing or thinking *at that moment*."

34 Stay Limber!

Would you sign up for a fitness class with an instructor who barks out exercise moves while slouching in a recliner and snacking on candy bars and potato chips? Not likely! Would you take your car to a mechanic who holds a wrench in one hand and a copy of *Quick and Easy Car Repair for Amateurs* in the other? Hire a car salesman who doesn't know a shingle from a showroom to repair the roof of your home? Pay good money to take a university chemistry class from a professor who wrote her thesis on Victorian poets? No, no, and no!

We expect those who provide a service to have expertise in that area and to be equipped to meet that specific need. The same applies to teachers: kids expect you to speak from experience when you teach—to "walk your talk," as we say. Christian teachers, more than any others, must speak from their hearts so as not to bring dishonor to God's name.

Do you want your children to grow and learn? Be sure that you are a model of growing and learning yourself. "The effective teacher always teaches from the overflow of a full life," writes Christian educator Howard Hendricks. "The Law of the Teacher, simply stated, is this: *If you stop growing today, you stop teaching tomorrow*" (*Teaching to Change Lives*).

You're on a journey—and you have not arrived at its end! As long as you are still breathing, there is something out there left to learn, some way left in which you can grow. It has nothing to do with age, and everything to do with attitude. The hunger you have for learning will be contagious—your kids will catch it from you. It's a great "condition" to spread!

Have you thought about all of the ways you can grow? Here are just a few:

- *Grow in biblical knowledge and understanding.* Scripture is where your beliefs and Christian life are shaped. Nourish your soul with God's Word every day.
- *Grow in community.* Your community of faith is a great source of challenge, encouragement, and understanding. God's church is a body, and its members are meant to attend to each other's needs. Become

part of a class, a small group, a prayer cell, or a task force so that God's people can keep you limber—and stretch you!

- *Grow new skills.* Even the most experienced teachers can benefit from further training. Take advantage of conferences, seminars, and workshops for techniques and skills that will improve your teaching and give you new insights into ways you can influence the children you teach.
- *Grow in knowledge.* Read books and magazines or surf the web to learn more about children's development, new curriculum approaches, and the latest information about the amazing world we live in. Acquiring new ideas and information will make you a better teacher.
- *Grow in grace.* The best teachers realize just how much they still have to learn. Seeking grace for the journey suggests that you are teachable.

The last word on growing belongs to the lifelong learner, the apostle Paul: "We pray that you'll live well for the Master, making him proud of you as you work hard in his orchard. As you learn more and more how God works, you will learn how to do your work" (Colossians 1:10, *The Message*).

35 Sharing Your Story

Every person who's ever lived has a story to tell. That's because life, as psychologist Erik Erikson has pointed out (see chapter 3, age level chart) is a series of challenges and struggles that need to be resolved as we grow and learn. And whenever there are problems to be solved, there is a story to tell!

The Bible is full of stories that show how God interacted with people. That same God is alive and well—still interacting with his people. As one of those people, you've got a story to tell too. Your story has chapters about lessons learned, grace experienced, failures overcome, and identity discovered. And whenever you share any part of your unique story with your kids, good things will happen:

- *It builds community.* Stories reveal to each other what we have in common. "When you can tell me your story, and I can bring to it my own feelings, my own past, my own peculiar way of seeing things, then your story can speak to where I live. I may change it around a bit in the process. If you can accept my doing that, then your story becomes a precious gift to me, and I can make it truly my own," writes Ralph Milton in *The Gift of Story* (Wood Lake Books, 1982).
- *It reveals universal truths.* Some have said there are only a very limited number of original stories in the world; the rest are all variations on grand themes. The story of how you made a mistake and received forgiveness is a universal story of grace; your story of a struggle that resulted in victory is a variation on the story of persistence winning out (remember Jesus' story of the persistent widow and the judge?). Each story you tell has the power to reinforce God's eternal truths for your kids.
- *It helps make abstract truths real.* You can teach all kinds of theological truths, but usually they won't impact kids as much as a personal story well told. We can tell our children that Jesus loves and saves us, but that may remain an abstraction until we tell them the story of how Jesus saved *us*. That's the point at which it becomes a truth that touches their hearts and makes it real!

- *It helps kids use their imaginations.* As you tell them your story, they'll begin to use their imaginations to recreate the events in their minds' eye. The more senses your listeners use, the better your teaching will "stick."
- *It will help you grow!* Every time you share a story about your own faith journey, you'll relive an experience that reminds you of God's grace and goodness, and you'll be strengthened—and grateful. You may notice new details that you hadn't thought of before, and the story will deepen your own faith.

Sessions in *Dwell* will invite you, time and time again, to share a part of your own story with the children. You might wonder if your own story is exciting enough or interesting enough to appeal to them. Perhaps you don't have a dramatic "testimony" about how you came to Christ—but that's precisely why it is important to share it! "I get the feeling that I can never be a first-class Christian because my sins are not exciting enough," writes Milton, reflecting on some dramatic testimonies he's heard. For the most part, life is *not* a mountain-top experience full of spine-tingling drama. When you tell your own quiet story, you might well be relieving many children of unrealistic expectations for their own faith experience.

Whenever you share your story of faith, remember to

- pray as you prepare, asking God's help in choosing what to say and how to say it.
- add simple visual effects if you have them—a photo of yourself as a child, the Bible your grandma used, a rock from the beach where you were baptized.
- be real. Children can quickly tell if you are making something up.
- lead the way. If you want children to talk about their own stories, you should be the model for them.
- refrain from adding a moral to the story. Let your story stand on its own. Children will add their own meaning, and it will be what God meant for them to understand.
- keep it short. Long stories may be too involved, too full of details, to appeal to kids.

Perhaps you feel somewhat shy about telling stories based on your own faith journey. A good place to begin is in your teachers' meetings or with a prayer partner. To jumpstart the process, ask each other questions like, "Tell about a time when you realized God was close to you" or "Share a story about a time when you learned a hard lesson." When you tell your story to a "safe" group, you will experience the wonderful growth in community that comes from sharing your story—and you'll be more likely to try it out with your kids.

When God told the Israelites to tell their stories to their children at mealtimes or bedtime or walking down the road, he had a purpose in mind. And like those ancient people of God, we join a long line of storytellers who are accomplishing God's purposes.

36
Finding Support

To grow properly, climbing roses, grapevines, and pole beans all need some kind of support structure. Shorter plants get support from digging their roots deep in the soil, and ground cover plants are supported by the earth itself as they creep across the soil or over rocks.

Sunday school teachers are a lot like those plants. Without support they'll dry up, wither away, and disappear. Sounds pretty harsh, right? But that's the way it is with ministry. Jesus said, "I am the vine, and you are the branches." In other words, if we want to bear fruit, we need divine support—and a human support system as well.

- *We need to be connected to God*, the source of all life and strength. Without God, we cannot bear fruit. Nothing can replace a living, growing relationship with God. Though you'll experience times of dryness and feelings of discouragement on your faith journey, know that God will never disconnect you from his love and support. If you're in a dormant stage right now, cling to God and you will, in time, discover new sap running through you.
- *We need to be connected to a spiritual community*. The church as the body of Christ has a role to play in supporting our ministry. Each of us is just one small part of the greater body; we need others to complement our gifts and keep us accountable. Your congregation should be supporting you with soul-refreshing worship and sacraments, prayer, financial and physical resources, mentoring and training, and with great love and gratitude for you and your contributions. If that's not happening, ask for it! You need this kind of support.
- *We need to be connected to the other members of our* Dwell *team*. Together we are stronger than the sum of our fellow teachers. Together we have a common goal that is easier to reach when we work with each other's gifts and talents. Being together is much more fun than trying to carry the load alone. So attend those teachers' meetings. You'll refresh and inspire each other and learn new things that will help you in your teaching. Share your classroom problems and seek advice.

Encourage others by affirming their gifts—the cheerful attitude that encourages you, the leadership that supports you, the musical talents that uplift you. Share the ideas, insights, and strategies that have worked for you. Pray and plan together for the best program possible for the children of your church.

- *Attend workshops, seminars/webinars, and conferences*; read books, magazines, websites, and newsletters—these are all tools for self-help and improvement. If you are eager to see learning, growing children in your classes, then be a model for them: use every opportunity to learn and grow yourself. *Dwell* offers its own teacher support and encouragement—check out the resources at www.dwellcurriculum.org.
- *Sometimes we need the kind of support and refreshment that comes through just having fun.* Although it seems counterproductive to take time off, fun and games and recreation are vital sources of support. They offer balance to keep you on an even keel. According to research, laughter lowers stress hormones, boosts immune response, increases creativity, oxygenates the blood, fosters positive energy and connections, and more (check out www.globalbellylaugh.com). Recreational activities such as hobbies, sports, travel, and fun with friends are all life-enriching experiences that take our minds off everyday problems and invite us to re-create ourselves.

How's your support system working? Have you established a personal network of individuals and groups who will be there when you need them? Are you grafted securely into the vine that is Jesus? When your support system includes divine and human connections, you'll continue to grow and flourish!

37
Holy Habits

Teaching is not all about us—it's about our great God and the children we're teaching and reaching for him. If our own faith grows and deepens in the process, that's wonderful! But if that *doesn't* happen for the kids we meet with each week, we haven't reached our goals.

Is the following statement true or false? *If only we can teach kids to believe the tenets of our faith, they'll live and act like children of faith.* Sounds good on paper maybe, but living the faith is not as simple as believing the right things. People who believe gluttony is a sin still overeat—and those who believe murder is evil still kill others with their unkindness and sharp words!

Teaching children means sharing the truth of Scripture with them—but it's even more important to give them opportunities to put what they believe into practice. Children who learn to live their faith when they're young have a head start on developing holy habits that stay with them long after you have moved out of their lives.

Here are some suggestions for helping your kids "walk the talk":

- *Don't be too quick to give kids ready answers.* Though it feels tidy to sum up your lesson each week with a single truth or moral, that may not be the most helpful to the children. Instead, ask good questions that nudge them to think for themselves. Motivate them to think about how they can apply what they've learned to their lives in the coming week. Challenge them to go deeper into the story, living out its truth. Instead of saying, "We've learned from the story of Ananias and Sapphira that Jesus is unhappy when we lie, so let's please Jesus by being truthful from now on" ask, "When are you tempted to lie? What could you do the next time you're in that situation?"
- *Use role play to help your kids "practice" an answer or application.* Though the situation may be artificial, role play allows kids to try answers on for size, fitting them to their experience and preparing them for future action. Instead of saying, "Today when you go home, try to do something that shows your family you love them"

say, "Before we leave, let's practice what we'll do to show love to our families. Choose a partner, and then tell each other what you'll do."

- *Rather than speaking in generalities, encourage your kids to make specific commitments.* Invite them to affirm what they believe by agreeing to act in concrete ways in the week ahead; follow up by talking about how they kept the commitments they made. Instead of saying, "Each of us should think about something we can do and report back next week" say, "For the next five minutes, write about (or draw) one thing you'll do differently this week. Put your commitment in an envelope with your name on it. Before we leave the room, we'll pray about your commitments; next week we'll open them and see how we've done."

38

Leading Children to Christ

When all is said and done, doesn't our ministry to children boil down to our hope and prayer that the children we teach will commit to following Jesus for the rest of their lives—to be Christ's faithful servants?

Researcher George Barna points out that most people who call themselves Christians say they committed their lives to Christ before they turned thirteen. They are responding to Jesus' invitation "Let the children come to me!" Some of the children you spend time with every week may even ask you questions about taking this big step in their lives. What an awesome privilege to be used by God in this way!

But it's also an awesome responsibility. Jesus warned adults who interact with kids not to cause them to stumble in the process of coming to Jesus. If you're wondering about the nature of your role and about just how you can help a child make a commitment to Jesus, you'll want to pay attention to the following guidelines:

- *Be sensitive to how you motivate children to take this step.* Kids are very impressionable—and they love to please the adults in their lives. It would be easy but wrong to put pressure on a child to make this serious, lifetime commitment before he or she is ready. "A faith community should never be involved in manipulating the soul of a child," writes Ivy Beckwith in *Postmodern Children's Ministry* (Zondervan, 2004). Children should only commit their lives to Christ in response to the work of the Holy Spirit, not because they want to please a teacher, go along with what their friends are doing, or fear eternal punishment. Pressure or fear can mislead children and stunt their relationship with our gracious and loving God.
- *Don't overlook or minimize a child's expressed desire to follow God's call.* Sometimes, in our efforts not to manipulate children, we might miss or even discount a child's response to the Spirit. "When children are told that Jesus wants to be their special friend and Savior, some will be ready to enter that relationship," writes Christian Education professor Catherine Stonehouse in *Joining Children on*

the Spiritual Journey (Baker, 1998). "They simply need a setting for response and possibly an adult to guide them, pray with them, and affirm their encounter with God."

- *Help children understand that personal commitment to Christ is a vital part of everyone's spiritual journey.* A child who is part of a faith community and participates in the life of the church probably sees herself as a follower of Christ. Because she's immersed in a Christian environment, it seems like part of her DNA. Teachers can affirm and support that identity, encouraging it to mature until the child is ready to make a personal commitment and claim that identity as her own. Watch for teachable moments for helping children in your group understand this process!
- *Partner with parents in nurturing their children's faith.* Parents have primary responsibility for nurturing their children's faith. But not all are committed to this God-given responsibility. When children in your group who have not grown up in the church tell you they want to accept Jesus as their Savior, be sure to communicate with their family about their decision. If the children are older, encourage them to share their thoughts and intentions with their family.
- *Partner with the entire community of faith.* A child who makes or reaffirms a commitment to Christ is also making a commitment to Christ's body, the church. You're part of a team that cares deeply about the spiritual growth of that child. Ask your pastor and other church leaders and members of the congregation to work with you to enfold the child with warmth and the love of Christ.

God extends his love and grace to us and promises never to leave us stranded in our faith journey, no matter what missteps we might make along the way. That grace applies to us as we lead children to Christ as well. It's helpful—and comforting—to remember that our faith walk is far more than a one-time, public commitment to Christ and the church. It's a lifelong journey. Take joy in helping kids take their first steps!

39

No Easy "How-to's"

Each child's faith journey is unique. And each teacher's relationship with children is different. When you seek to lead children to Jesus, no formula will replace the guidance of God's Spirit as you respond to Jesus' command from Matthew 19: "Let the little children come to me. . ." The following questions and answers cover issues you may bc wondcring about.

- *What is my role in this process?* Only God's mysterious work can truly influence a child to make a commitment to Jesus. Your role as a leader is to present God's welcoming message and to model your own faith by
  - praying for the children in your group.
  - presenting the good news to them.
  - welcoming questions . . . any questions!
  - answering questions honestly . . . even if it means saying "I don't know."
  - telling your own story.
  - helping a child respond to the Holy Spirit's nudge.
  - remaining alert to indications that children want to "go deeper."
- *How do I know when a child is ready to make a commitment to Jesus?* For starters, pray, observe, ask questions.
  - *Pray* that God will usc you to lead others to him. Pray that your message will find fertile soil. Pray for the needs of your children and ask God to give you ears to listen.
  - *Observe* your kids closely. Those who show a keen interest in learning more, those who ask probing questions, those who seek you out before or after class, those who say they'd like to know Jesus better—these are children who may be ready to make a commitment. But don't overlook those who are reticent or express doubts or fears—these kids too may be searching for a closeness to Jesus, a peace at the center of their lives.
  - *Ask* kids questions that gauge their relationship with God. This might be done best outside of class, in a child's home or some

public place. Remember always to partner with the child's parents. Keep questions simple, especially for younger children: How do you feel about Jesus? How do you think Jesus feels about you? What would you like to tell Jesus? You might ask older children to tell you in their own words what it means to follow Jesus. Can they tell you, in a simple way, what the heart of the gospel message is? Affirm their answers with this assurance from the apostle Paul: "If you declare with your mouth, 'Jesus is Lord,' and believe in your heart that God raised him from the dead, you will be saved" (Romans 10:9).

- *I'm pretty sure that one of the kids in my group is ready to make a commitment to Jesus. Now what?*
  - Pray with that child, encouraging him to pray too, asking Jesus to be his Savior and Lord. Suggest asking a parent (or other family member) or perhaps a friend to join you as you pray together. Or encourage the child to talk with his family later, telling them of his commitment. Better yet, go with him to share the good news!
  - Here's a way you could help a young child pray: *Dear Jesus, Thank you for loving me. I know I disobey you and do wrong things. I'm sorry. I know that God loves me and forgives my sins. I want to love you more. Amen.* Older children may prefer to write their own prayers, or they may ask you to suggest words for them to use. If they're shy or feel inadequate, offer to pray on their behalf after asking them what they'd like you to say in the prayer.

Making a commitment to Christ is a big step, but it's not the end of the road. There are many steps to come. Encourage kids who've made this choice as they continue to follow Jesus, step by step by step:

- Give a younger child a Bible storybook that reinforces the good news of Jesus' love. Or suggest a book the child's family might use for devotions.
- Encourage older children to spend time with Jesus by reading their Bible and praying. You might give them a Bible if they don't already have one or a devotional book to help them get started. Encourage them to attend worship and participate in the Lord's Supper. Remind them too that there will always be more to learn about Jesus and his love—that's why Sunday school is so important.

- If the child isn't baptized and would like to join the church, talk with the family about the child's desire.

Don't forget to celebrate! Celebrate the gifts the child brings to Christ's body and encourage ways to use those gifts (see ch. 40). Celebrate the Spirit's work in that child's heart, and rejoice with God's people in your faith community!

40

Growing Kids' Gifts

You've probably heard well-intended church people say things like "We need to train our children well—they're the church of the future" or "Let's use music that appeals to our kids; after all, they're tomorrow's church."

Not so! Children' aren't the church of tomorrow—they're the church of today just as much as adults are! There's no magic moment at which people become old enough to "be the church." In fact, as we know, Jesus more than once reminded the folks of his day that children are the greatest in his kingdom.

We'd do well to read and reread 1 Corinthians 12 to remind ourselves what it means to be many parts, but one body—and then to apply Paul's words to the children among us in a way that nudges us to look for their particular gifts to the body. For example, when a four-year-old kisses the cast on a senior's broken leg, she's putting to good use her gifts of mercy, healing, and encouragement. And when a seven-year-old responds to the pastor's question during the children's message, he's using his gift of wisdom and discernment. A ten-year-old's comments and questions about a divisive denominational issue might cause adults to reconsider their own dogmatic opinions on both sides. You've probably got your own stories about similar ways in which the kids in your congregation—and your Sunday school class—have deepened your faith.

Here are some ways you can help kids identify, develop, and use their gifts for the benefit of the body:

- *Be an encourager.* Many people learn about their spiritual gifts when others notice them and offer encouragement: "You're an excellent helper, Pete!" or "You ask the most interesting questions, Julie—you really make me think." Such comments alert kids to the gifts God's Spirit has given them and encourage kids to use those gifts.
- *Be a facilitator.* In your work with children, you'll notice strengths and gifts that may be less obvious to others in the congregation. If a child in your group has drawn a particularly moving picture of the crucifixion or written an especially beautiful poem, find ways of sharing

these gifts with the rest of the congregation by posting them on a bulletin board or giving them to the church newsletter editor for publication. You might also come across ways your kids can serve or put their gifts to good use on church projects, work Saturdays, and in worship. Consider yourself the link!

- *Be a teacher.* Introduce the idea of spiritual gifts (and the language used to describe them) to your kids by incorporating it into your storytelling and teaching. You can do this by naming the gifts of people in the Bible and talking about how they used them for the Lord and his people. Share historical and contemporary stories of Christians who've used their gifts to build up the church.
- *Be a model.* Remind yourself that you are gifted too! Are you serving God's kingdom with joy? Are you nurturing your own gifts and using them ever more effectively through new learning? Are you relying on the Holy Spirit to see you through the challenges? Are you seeking support, prayer, and encouragement from God's family to deepen and strengthen your commitment?

Consider these encouraging words from Jesus himself: "Whoever welcomes one such child"—*his or her smile, energy, creativity, loving spirit, helpfulness, inquisitiveness*—"in my name welcomes me" (Matthew 18:5). That's exactly what you're doing when you help the kids in your group *be the church*—today!

41 Pass It On!

Ready for some good news? You're not alone—there's a whole group of wannabe teachers in your room who are ready to share the teaching load. That would be your kids! It may not make mathematical sense, but here's a good equation to remember: 2 teach is 2 learn 2 times!

Here's another way to express it: When your kids have opportunities to practice their learning by teaching others, they learn even more.

In his book *Help! I'm a Sunday School Teacher!* (Youth Specialties, 1995) Ray Johnston lists further benefits that come from giving your children an opportunity to do some of the teaching:

- It combats apathy. Kids who are actively involved don't have a chance to become bored or disruptive.
- Children (especially older ones) often listen better to other children than they do to adults.
- Being placed in a teaching role can help kids discover potential gifts of leadership and teaching.

Start small by inviting kids to take turns praying, choosing songs, reading Scripture, and doing other things you'd normally do. Give specific instructions ahead of time and be sure kids understand that you're counting on them. You might say, "Maria, I'd like you to lead the opening litany next week. Here are the words—please take them home and practice them this week."

Review activities also provide a good opportunity for kids to try their hand at teaching. Invite them to retell stories in their own words and to create visual aids to accompany the stories. Look for lots of ways to invite children into review activities: writing story questions, composing review quizzes, serving as referees for games of Bible baseball, operating audiovisual equipment, and more.

Don't forget that teaching is not limited to words. Skills such as art, music, drama, and social interaction are learned through observation and imitation. Assign partners in ways that benefit both—pair a weaker reader with a stronger one, a social child with a shy one, a "wild child" with one who's more disciplined, an artist with a child less gifted in that area, and so on. As pairs work together on projects or assignments, they'll become models and helpers for each other.

Occasionally challenge kids with specific assignments too. For example, if you ask children to bring items for a food bank, ask one or two kids to be in charge of publicity, making posters and writing a notice for the bulletin; others might create a goal chart and track donations; others might be in charge of signing up drivers and arranging for deliveries.

Take a risk; share the load. At the very least, kids will gain new appreciation for your job and all it involves. Chances are, your efforts will communicate to the children in your group that they indeed are the church—right now!

In his book *Theology of Children's Ministry* (Zondervan, 1983), church education specialist Lawrence Richards suggests that children are most likely to embrace faith and make it their own if they receive the following from their church:

- A sense of belonging: "This is my church, and I'm valued here."
- An opportunity to participate in the ministries of the church: "I can do something for God."
- Faith models: "The people in this church are showing me how to serve God."
- Opportunities to learn about faith outside the Sunday school class: "My faith grows when I serve at the soup kitchen or help clean up the parking lot."
- Teaching about making good choices—and support in making them: "I can learn how to say no to temptations; if I fail, someone will help me figure out how to do better next time."

These are ideals we all aspire to. The following are some creative, practical suggestions, gathered from those who know and care, for incorporating them into the life of the church:

- Invite kids to create bulletin covers or brochures to advertise children's ministries offered by your church.
- Invite seniors to a special *Dwell* session; pair them with children and invite the seniors to show kids pictures of their youth and share their stories.

- Include in your church's newsletter or on its website pictures of kids and teachers in their *Dwell* sessions.
- Invite children to help deacons pass offering baskets.
- Form a group of children who pray for sick members of your congregation.
- Pair fifth- and sixth-graders with mentors who get to know them and meet regularly to share stories and talk about faith.
- Invite children to take turns providing snacks for and interacting with another group in your congregation (for example, a Friendship Group made up of members who have cognitive disabilities).
- If your church provides nametags for members, make sure kids have them as well as adults.
- Provide children's bulletins aimed at helping kids understand and participate in worship.
- Invite families to take turns baking (or bringing) bread for communion.
- Make sure coffee *and juice* are served during the fellowship hour.
- Introduce a question box for kids' questions; ask the pastor to read/answer them in worship from time to time.
- Hold an annual "Creation Care" service outdoors, followed by a guided hike.
- Encourage church committees to include a member who's a child, or to solicit kids' input on some of their decisions.
- Start a church garden on the grounds and involve kids in its care and harvest; give the produce to a food bank.
- Plan an intergenerational church retreat.

Not bad for starters! You've probably got other suggestions for incorporating kids into the full life of your congregation. As a *Dwell* teacher, you're an advocate for this process. Grab the opportunity and rejoice in the results—it's a way of building God's kingdom.

42
Looking Back, Looking Ahead

Robert Raikes (1735-1811) has often been called "Mr. Sunday School." Raikes noticed how little opportunity there was for children of working class parents to receive an education (because at that time many children joined their parents in the workforce from Monday through Saturday). So in 1780, he set up a *Sunday* school in his hometown of Gloucester, England. It was a place where kids could learn to read and write—using the Bible as a textbook.

By 1831 the movement Raikes had begun had spread across England, reaching and teaching 1.25 million children—one-quarter of all English children. Sunday school changed kids' lives, teaching them spiritual truths along with the skills of reading and writing.

Sunday school has had a long tradition of helping people grow, change, and meet life's challenges. It has been an outreach program for children who've never heard about Jesus' saving love; a support system to help parents teach their children Scripture and spiritual truth; and a child-oriented ministry in an adult-dominated menu of church programs. It's also been a safe haven for battle-weary children, a place where Christian beliefs are woven into the fabric of their lives. Hymns and melodies first learned in Sunday school have comforted soldiers in battle, elderly Christians in rest homes, and patients in hospital beds.

What will the Sunday school of the future be like? No one really knows—but it's interesting to look at the possibilities in the light of our culture today. It's a reality the church must understand as it plans its ministries to children. In her book *Today's Sunday School: Dead or Alive?* Margaret F. Williamson describes the effects of today's world on the lives of our kids:

- Our consumer-driven culture creates trends such as *cocooning* (the stay-at-home trend), *clanning* (the desire to be together with like-minded people), and *anchoring* (reaching back to spiritual roots).

- Busyness and multiple roles are a fact of life. Time is even more important than money. Sunday school has to fit into a schedule beset by time constraints.
- Society is reinventing itself every three to five years. Change is inevitable, not an option.
- The population of North America is changing, with diversity rather than homogeneity becoming the norm.
- Family structures are changing: the nuclear family (working dad, stay-at-home mom, a few children) comprises less than 10 percent of the population. Single-parent households are growing quickly.
- The church is no longer considered the only authority in the search for spiritual truth. The Internet, books, television, non-Christian traditions, and personal experiences are alternate sources.

(Check out the *Journal for Baptist Theology and Ministry* (vol 1, Fall 2003, pp. 122-139) www.baptistcenter,com/Journal for an expanded version of this material.)

What are the implications of this new reality for the children to whom we minister? Perhaps the kids in your group come from a variety of ethnic groups and family situations. Attendance may be irregular because of visitation rights in divorce situations, sports practices and competitions, or the sheer overload of busy work weeks and the need to "catch up" that Sundays offer. You may have children in your class whose parents or caregivers are checking out "church" for the first time ever—and you wonder how to encourage them to return, much less support your ministry to their child by following up on stories or memory work.

Besides being labeled as Millennials or the Net Generation, the kids in your group have also been dubbed "the mosaic generation"—a generation of children characterized by nonlinear thinking. That means they are used to picking up information in bits and pieces, fitting everything into spaces in their minds, but not necessarily connecting everything logically. Their thinking is influenced by fast movies, fast video games, fast changes in society. Kids have become comfortable with contradictions; they're not especially concerned with absolute truths. How do you reach and teach them? By forming relationships with them so that they come to know and trust you. By becoming comfortable with and using the technology that's second nature for them. By using the music and language of their world. Not by lectures.

Imagine a Sunday school approach that meets the needs of today's kids. It needs to be fun and varied, using a variety of activities, technology, and music that speaks to them. It requires teachers who are warm and caring, who are unafraid of being authentic and vulnerable, who are willing to keep in touch with kids outside of the classroom by whatever technology they're using. Sunday school needs to be intergenerational too, so that kids are exposed to role models and receive spiritual mentoring from people of all ages and stages in their own faith journeys. More than ever before, kids need a classroom atmosphere that's safe and secure, in which they feel free to ask questions and explore possible answers.

Culture changes—but kids' basic needs do not. So take heart when critics scorn the institution of Sunday school and predict its demise. Sunday school matters—and your ministry to children matters. You're passing on God's Story to God's kids, and you're doing it Jesus' way—with warmth, acceptance, and love. Thank you!